GLOBAL GREEN BOOK

HIGHLIGHTING BLACK FRIENDLY PLACES

HEALTHCARE EDITION

Publisher
BillMari Inc

Edited by
Sinclair Skinner and Akua N. Zenzele

Compiled by
Yvonne Dushime

www.iloveblackpeople.com | www.BillMari.com

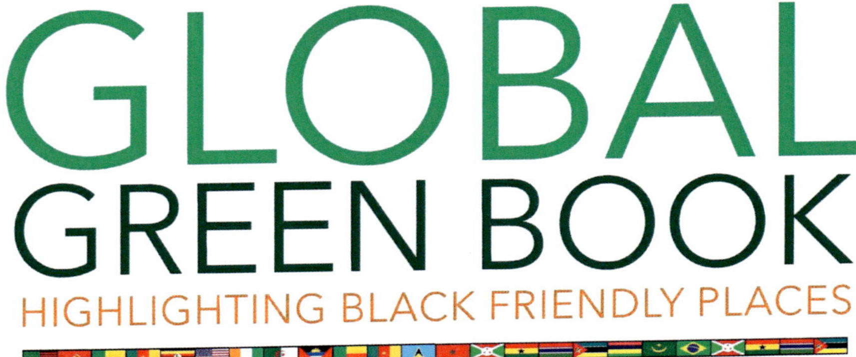

For your continued Support, Participation,
Recommendations, Contributions & Prayers, we say

Asante (Thank You).

Shukrani kwa Mwenyezi Mungu to our ***Ancestors,***

Asanteni to our Ambassadors, Asanteni to our ***Founding* Members**,

Asanteni to our **Members, *Asanteni*** to the many interns

that joined our team, ***Asanteni*** to our Project Partners…

Asanteni To our ***Healthcare Providers,***

Asanteni To **our Families and Friends**, ***Asanteni***

Humbly dedicated to all those we lost during this global pandemic

TABLE OF CONTENTS

Chapter 1: Directories of Healthcare Providers

This is a small sample of available recommendations.
To find, add or correct, go to **www.iloveBlackpeople.com**

The Global Green Book
A Black Survival Guide

Holistic Healers

Dr. Pamela (Yewong) Hall-Black Owned
Acupuncture, Chinese Herbs, Reiki, Tantra Instructor, Cryoskin Weight Management
Baltimore, MD
443-824-3487

Sheila Hall-Black Owned
Unique Scripts Wellness
Wellness Spa, Herbals, Nutritional Therapy, Reflexology
Randallstown, MD
410-913-7448
www.SheilaLHall.com / www.EistrongHerbal.com

Yuma "Docta Yew" Bellamee-Black Owned
Holistic Practitioner/Herbalist
Washington, DC
202-469-0264

Sandy Woods-Black Owned Herbalist/Detox Services/Traditional Healer Baltimore, MD
410-294-4555
www.detoxwithsandy.com

Willis Jasper a.k.a Baba Fadare-Black Owned
Acupuncture, Qi Gong, Chinese/Japanese Healing Modalities, Traditional Healer Art of Wellness Baltimore, MD
443-527-2713
artsofwellness@yahoo.com

Thema Azize Serwaa The Womb Sauna
Womb Health, Traditional Healer 888-576-9662
www.wombsauna.com

Traditional Life Ministries, Inc. -Black Owned
Wellness Classes on Traditional Herbalism and Self-Healing/Wellness Retreats; Traditional/Spiritual Heali Services, Spiritual Healing Baths
410-435-9647
www.TraditionalLifeMinistries.org

Nilajah Brown-Black Owned
The Birth Well
Childbirth Consultations,
Childbirth and Yoga Classes, Doula Services
Baltimore, MD
443-803-8103

Heather Clark-Black Owned
Traditional Healer, Shaman
Baltimore, MD
443-939-1465

Haleem Abdul-Rahman-Black Owned
Wellness Coach
Baltimore, MD
410-499-5982

Coach Howard Falcon-Black Owned
Physical Trainer, Fitness Coach Baltimore, MD
443-635-2264

Navasha Daya-Black Owned Reiki Master, Traditional Healer Baltimore, MD
443-850-5816

Ishmael Murray-Black Owned
Herbalist, TraditionalPriest/Healer
Baltimore, MD
410-299-5858

Joshua Lee, LCSW-C-Black Owned Social Worker, Mental HealthTherapist Baltimore, MD
443-939-6518

Iya Olosunde Ifatooke Ajala-Black Owned
Yoni Steam Institute Womb Health, Reiki Master Healer, TraditionalPriest/Healer New York, NY
804-596-9664

Avalaura Gaither-Black Owned
Avalaura's Healing Center
Reiki Master, Wellness/Life Coach 301-458-0335
www.avalaurahealing.com

Dr. Rosemary Cook, PhD, LCSW-C-Black Owned
Totally Whole Pastoral Counseling Services, LLC
Psychologist, mental health therapist Baltimore, MD
(410) 346-2035

Mamatoto Village-Black Owned
Maternity Care, Doula Services,
Pregnancy/Pos tpartum, Breastfeeding Support,
Parenting Support
Washington, DC 20019
202-248-3434
www.Mamatotovillage.org

DancerFit by Dionne-Black Owned Dance and Fitness Classes Washington, DC 20011 202-681-0419
dancerfitbydionne@gmail.com

Dr. Terry Victor-Black Owned
Dentist (Direct-Pay/Cash Only)
Washington, DC
202-544-3626
www.theDCdentist.com

Dr. Akua Gray-Black Owned
A Life of Peace Wellness Institute Naturopath, Traditional Priest/HealerClasses, Trainings, Healing Services
Missouri, TX
832-303-3277/ 713-893-8447
www.alifeofpeace.org

Thema Aziz Serwa-Black Owned
The Womb Sauna,Womb Health,
Women Empowerment, Vaginal Dialogues Facilitator Bowie, MD
www.thewombsauna.com

Divine Doula Goddess-Black Owned Doula and Spiritual Services Fayetteville, NC
910-502-3936

Iya Oyawunmi Ajala-Black Owned
Traditional Priest/Healer
216-466-2939
www.ilearira.com

Mama Ife Fatiu-Black Owned
Birthing Doula, Lactation Specialist, Kemetic Yoga, Relationship Counselor, Breathologist
Baltimore, MD
www.Plm95.org
nommoservices@gmail.com

BOOMBox Boxing Club-Black Owned
Boxing/Fitness Club Washington,
DC 20003
202-599-2799
Boombox-boxing.com

Belin Sport and Fitness-Black Owned
Sports and Fitness Club Washington,
DC 20002
202-702-7126
Bfitdc.net

Total Source Fitness Gym-Black Owned
Fitness Center/Gym Washington,
DC 20002 TotalSourceFitness.com

Haji Healing Salon-Black Owned Acupuncture, Yoga, Reiki, Classes, Apothecary Chicago, IL 60653
312-375-7445
www.hajihealing.com

Pearled Buddha, LLC-Black Owned Yoga, Doula Services, Life-Coach Service Gilbert, AZ
pearledbuddha@gmail.com
www.pearledbudha.com

HerbBae Naturals-Black Owned Health and Beauty Herbals, Massage
Herbbae.bigcartel.com

Dr. Tawainna Houston, ND, MDiv-Black Owned

Journey of Wellness Natural Medicine Center Naturopathic Doctor (404) 585-1561
DrTHouston.com

Hempress Farms, LLC-Black Owned
CBD Dispensary Hemp
Farm Winston-Salem,
NC 336-775-7663
www.hempresshealer.com

Dr. Winston Kokayi Patterson-Black Owned African Wholisitc Health Association Acupuncturist, Holistic Hea
Practitioner
Washington, DC
202-412-4880
Wpkokayi1@yahoo.com

Queen Afua Wellness Institute-Black Owned
Classes and courses for holistic wellness, healing products, books, Sacred Woman training
New York, NY
888-344-4325
www.QueenAfua.com

NatuREAL Essentials-Black Owned
Skin, Hair, Beauty and Home Herbals www.naturealessentials.com

It's Time for Healing Holistic & Fitness Sanctuary-Black Owned Womb Herbal
Steams, Natural Lippo, Doula Services, Herbals, Workshops and Retreats
Alexandria, VA 22310
www.itstimeforhealing.com

Skai Juice-Black Owned
Juice Cleanse, Products, Wholistic Wellness Chef www.SkaiJuice.com
abundance@skaijuice.com

The Green House Juice Café-Black Owned
Juice Bar and health food café
Baltimore, MD 21218
(410) 889-1391

Lon Don GH Fitness-Black Owned Gym, fitness, and training center Cape Coast, Ghana
+233 540 833 844/+233 541 891 171

Acupuncture by Stephanie-Black Owned
Healing Arts of Silver Spring, LLC Acupuncturist, Herbalist Silver Spring, MD 20910
(301) 585-2200

Black Veg Society-Black Owned
Special events, webinars, cooking demos, and wellness classes Baltimore, MD 21201
(410) 225-5874
www.blackvegsociety.org

Astral Healing Arts Wellness Center-Black Owned Yoga, Massage Therapy, Chakra Balancing, Reiki Hyattsville, MD
www.AstralHealingArts.com

CC Hunter-Jean, SAP, LCSW-Black Owned
Professional Counseling Services Gulfport, MS 39507
228-220-4226
www.getliftedgirl.org

Khetnu Nefer-Black Owned
A Soulful Touch Wellness, LLC
Massage Therapist, Women's Health Coach, Herbalist, Mobile holistic
Washington, DC 150
843-564-2464
www.asoulfultouch.com

About Colons Hydrotherapy and Wellness Center -Black Owned
Colon Therapist, Wellness Services Parkville, MD
21234
443-224-3639
www.AboutColons.com

Then The Sun Rose, LLC-Black Owned
Reiki, Coaching/Mentoring, Healing
Retreats, Workshops 708-824-
8443
www.thenthesunrose.com

Mindful Home Interiors-Black Owned
Wellness Counseling (support through grief, loss and difficult life transitions) Wake Forest, NC
27587
919-229-9152
www.mindfulhomeinteriorsnc.com

Liberation Health Strategies-Black Owned Health
blog, Yoga, Healer
www.liberationhealthstrategies.com

Princess Akeema Holistic Health, LLC-Black Owned
Natural Health Exam, Ear candling, Private
Yoga Sessions, Reflexology,
Ionic Foot Detox, Aromatherapy, Yoni Steam Catonsville,
MD 21228
(443) 873 0532
www.princessakeema.com

Denis Ausar Winkler-Black Owned
TNAT Holistic Wellness Center, LLC Psychotherapist Baltimore MD,
21214
410-777-5020 www.TNAT-HWC.com

Ausar Winkler
Sifu/ Medical Tai Chi and QI Gong and
Mixed Martial Arts Instructor Baltimore
MD, 21214
410-777-5020
www.TNAT-HWC.com

Albert Phillips, Sr-Black Owned
Mental Health Therapist Baltimore, MD
433-415-5384

Growing Boundlessly-Black Owned
Mental health services
(parenting challenges, depression, trauma, stress, body image, self-esteem) Chicago, IL 152
312-577-7258
www.growingboundlessly.com

Jamila Jones Clinical Counseling and Consulting, LLC-Black Owned Mental health services (recovery from pain, fear, addiction and more) Chicago, IL 60615
312-451-9230
www.jamilajoneslcpc.com

Scent-Sational Touch: A Healing Indulgence-Black Owned
Hand-crafted herbals, soaps and more
Brooklyn, NY www.scentsationaltouch.com

Custom Creations Consulting and Training-Black Owned
Doula Services, Life Coach, Herbalist Baltimore, MD
443-402-5544

Herbal Creations by Akua-Black Owned
Hand- crafted herbals (skin, hair and bath products) 410-435-9647
www.HerbalCreationsByAkua.com

Thema Azize Serwaa-Black Owned
Womb Health, Traditional Healer The Womb Sauna 888-576-9662 www.wombsauna.com

Mother's Nature-Black Owned
CBD-Infused Skincare
301-204-4505, 504-502-7217
www.mothersnature.net

Nyambi Naturals, LLC-Black Owned Urban Apothecary, Plant-Powered Beauty Philadelphia, PA 19120
267-736-1986
www.nyambinatural.com

Shani Adia Yoga, LLC-Black Owned Yoga classes www.shaniadiayoga.com

Isis Wellness Bar-Black Owned
Yoni Steam, Prostate Steam, Facials,Body Treatments, Waxing Services, Body Contouring
Knightdale, NC 27545
919-752-6513
www.isiswellnessbar.com

Ima Paz-Webb, M.S., LCPC, NCC-Black Owned
SMR Counseling Services, LLC
Clinical Mental Health Specialist
Burtonsville, MD 20866
(240) 389-1487

Institute for Healing, LLC-Black Owned
Holistic mental health services Owings Mills, MD 21117
(410) 864-0211
www.ihealmd.com

SMR Counseling Services, LLC-Black Owned
Counseling services(marital/ premarital, grief/loss, depression, stress management, anger management, parenting support)
Burtonsville, MD 20866
(240) 389-1487

Black Male Yoga Initiative-Black Owned
Yoga, Guided Meditation
443-519-2251
www.bmyi.org

Alycea K. Shirley-Black Owned
The Wellness House of Healing
Massage Therapy (specializing medical massage and cupping therapy) Bronx, NY/ Accra, Ghana
347-435-8393

Red Hot Yoga Smyrna-Black Owned Hot Yoga (Hatha, Vinyasa, Yin) Smyrna, GA 30080
404-840-1410
www.redhotyogasmyrna.com

Dr Philip Nicolas-Black Owned
Chiropractic Columbia, MD 21044
410-992-7730
https://www.towncenterchiropractic.com/

Dr. Willie Richardson-Black Owned
Holistic Dentistry Baltimore, MD 21215
(410) 542-6900

Dr. Marcus Allen-Black Owned
Chiropractor Baltimore,
MD 21202
(410) 244-0440

Intentional Healing Space-Black Owned Therapeutic
Service www.intentionalhealingspace.com
410 733-2055

Constance Glow-Black Owned
Esthetician www.constanceglow.com/

Gifts, LLC-Black Owned Mental
Health www.giftspsych.com/

Zanobia Abena-Black Owned
ZM Spa
Massage Therapy Ghana,
West Africa
+233 202701043
ZMSpa1@gmail.com

Vanessa Geffrard, MPH-Black Owned
Vagesteem
Workshops and Podcast around Vaginal Health/Empowernment and Sex Education
443-850-3800
Vagesteem@gmail.com
Vagesteem.com

Bikram Yoga Works/DRIP'T STUDIOS-Black Owned
Bikram Yoga Works Ivy City
Cryotherapy, PEMF Therapy,and Fascia Stretch Therapy Washington
D.C. 20002
info@bikramyogaworks.com
www.bikramyogawellnessworks.com

Dr. Dean Seneb El-Black Owned
Sankofa Chiropractic Wellness Centre Spinal Health, Back Pain, Waist Pain, Nerve & Vascular Pain, Massage & Fitness
Offshore Takoradi, Ghana
+233 552508872/+233 506038177
SankofaChiropractic@gmail.com

Candace J. Mickens, LMT-Black Owned
Sacred Touch Body Work, LLC Massage Therapy, Yoga 240-351-4198

Tenecia Brown-Black Owned
Oracle Oils, LLC
Luxurious, healing and healthy fragrances for body, mind and spirit (oils, butters, candles, body liquids) Baltimore, MD
Oracleoilsllc@gmail.com
Instagram-tbrowntheoracle

The Crystal Yogi-Black Owned
Trauma Informed Wellness,Yoga, Reiki, Healing Crystal Jewelry Odenton, MD
https://linktr.ee/ZohameansLight

Supreme Essence-Black Owned
Plant Food and Wellness
Retreats, Massage Therapy, Music and Sound Therapy, Spiritual Healing Services, Plant-based Coaching, Midwifery and Doula Services
Metro Atlanta, Georgia
(404) 436-1742
Info@supremeessencepfw.com https://w w w.supremeessencepfw.com

Dr. Mahipat Mediquest, LLC-Black Owned
Chiropractic Services Randallstown, MD
21133-6202, 410-655-8900
www.drmahipat.com

Hue Café Baltimore-Black Owned lant-based Café and Apothecary Owings Mills, MD 21117
443-352-3006
www.huecafebaltimore.com

Naomi Hanna Seshat's Permaculture-Black Owned permaculture Farming, Herbalism; classes and workshops **Lnktr.ee/seshatsbrush**

Sanahara Ama Chandra Brown-Black Owned Sound Healing, Reiki, Intuitive Spiritual Readings, Holistic Nursing, Quantum Energy Sessions Baltimore, MD
www.sanaharaenergetics.com

Wild Ginger Herbal Center-Black Owned
Community Herbal Center, online herbal and birthkeeper programs Costa Rica
Linktr.ee/wildgingerherbalcenter

The Stone Foundation Counseling Group-Black Owned
Counseling services (individual and group) for adults, children, families, couples and teens.
Towson, MD 21286
410-296-2004

Yeyefini Efunbolade-Black Owned
Yeyefini Balanced Living
Traditional Priestess/Healer, Diviner, Author Ft. Lauderdale, FL 33310
888-419-5848
www.Yeyefini.com

Nana Bosumfour Ayinsongya Azumah-Black Owned Traditional Healer
Tigari and Mmotia Priest, Herbalist Bogolatanga, Ghana (Upper East Region)
+233 24 5242714
+233 54 0501516

Delisa Worthy-Black Owned Reiki
Master and Trainer Baltimore, MD
443 677 3486

Fabienne G. Delacroix-Black Owned
Tantra Instructor
Miami, Florida 213
807 5527

Ausar Auset Society-Black Owned
Teaches breath techniques, African Spiritual Values,
Wholistic Health Food store owners, founders of the African Spiritual Coalition Washington, D.C.
202-723- 5200

Gwendolyn West-Black Owned Nurse,
Lactation and Birthing Specialist
wombfruit_birth_lactation@hotmail.com
gwest@huhosp.org

Ayo Hany-Kendi, The Breath Sekou-Black Owned
Certified Optimum Life Breathologists (COLB), Transformational Facilitator, Laughter Yoga Teacher, Reiki Master 3, Qigong II, RaSekhi, Life Coach, Sound Healer, Cultural Rituals Facilitator, Founder of Black Love Day- February 13 Capital Heights, MD
202-667-2577
ayomenasjoy@yahoo.com
www.PositiveEnergyWorks.com

Lona Alias aka Amoya-Black Owned
Meditation Master,Certified Optimum Life Breathologists (COLB), Spiritual Life Coach and Mystic
DC and Metropolitan Area 202-
270-2271

Dr. Karen Khadijah Davis-Foulks-Black Owned
Certified Lymphologist, Conscious Self Healthcare Educator, NES Health Certified Wellness Specialist in Informational Medicine, Founder of Emancipate Yourself from Medical Slavery Day-April 30
Washington, DC
202-248-7749
www.consciousSelfcare.com
www.4celllife.com
www.youtube.com/kdavisf

Manifest Ra-Black Owned
Qigong Master, Certified Optimum Life Breathologists (COLB) wholisticallyspeaking@hotmail.com

Rachel Pope-Black Owned
Relaxation Specialist, Art Therapist, Certified Optimum Life Breathologist (COLB) Washington, DC
202-679-1360

Tauhidi Salahuddin-Black Owned
Master in Yayasan Kalimasada (Indonesian Health and Healing techniques that include Breathing Techniques, Certified Optimum Life Breathologist (COLB) 703-321-6326
tauhidie@aol.com

Yirser Ra Hotep-Black Owned
Master Yoga Teacher, Khamitan (Egyptian) yoga Chicago, IL
773-908-7074
yirser@yogaskills.com

Brother Hawah-Black Owned
Yoga Instructor, Founder One Common Unity 202-529-2125
one@everlutionary.net

Dana Smith, The Yoga Diva-Black Owned
Yoga Master and Instructor, Founder of Divine Essence Yoga School Clinton, MD
301-952-9464
dmith@essenceyoga.net

Aaron K. Mottley, CHHC-Black Owned
Oxygen, Nutrition, Exercise Specialist, Breath Master, Certified Wholistic Practitioner, Certified Herbal consultant, Certified Kemetic Yoga Instructor Washington, DC
202-848-5448
www.internalfitnesstrainer.com

Montsho & Nwasha
Therapist, Founder Akoma Day and Akoma House Initiative
New Jersey akomahouseinitiative@gmail.com

Eliza Cooper-Black Owned
Therapist, Life Coach, Sponsors Black Love Events and Cultural parent Initiative
Baltimore, MD
410-404-2859
ParentLove@yahoo.com
LiveHolisticallyBalanced@gmail.com

Dr. Kevin Washington-Black Owned Psychiatrist, Cultural/Spiritual Counselor Mwata357@gmail.com

Wekesa O. Madzimoyo-Black Owned
Life Coach,Cultural Therapist
Atlanta, GA wekesa@gmail.com

BodyFlow Works-Black Owned
Yoga
Ghana, West Africa
+233 55 667 0800

Dr. Allison Henderson,DC-Black Owned
Chirpractor, Iridologist Washington, DC
20003
(202) 544-4478

The Noble Touch, Inc. -Black Owned
Energy Healing Services, Pranic Healing, Trainings,Community Programs,Individual Healing
New York, NY
877-493-9433
info@thenobletouch.org

Ifetayo White-Black Owned
Reiki Master 3, Doula Master, Healer,Yoga, Meditation Saint Helenes Island, NC https://insighttimer.com/ifetayowhite

Dr. Jewel Pookrum, MD, PhD-Black Owned
Master Physician and Holistic Healer in Mind/Body Medicine https://drjewelsbrainbalancingprogram.com/

George Love-Black Owned QiGong Master Teacher
Geolove49@gmail.com

Afro-Vegan Society-Black Owned
www.ActionNetwork.org info@afrovegansociety.org

Chef Keidi Odwuduo
Vegan Nutritionist and Chef, Author of Nutritional and Cultural Books, Founder/Broadcaster of LIBRadio www.ChefKeidi.com

Kathryn Davis-Black Owned
QiGong Teacher, Meditation, Energy Healing Brooklyn, NY
347-480-1694
Kathryn.one HeartOfMindRadio.com QiGongOnLine.net

Brown and Healthy-Black Owned
Global health and wellness initiative;
fitness classes, youth and adult wellness programs, community events
Los Angelos, CA / Baltimore, MD
www.brownandhealthy.com

Dr. Sharita Yazid, ND-Black Owned Naturopath, Herbalist, Iridologist, Nutritionist Los Angeles, CA/ Ghana, West Africa
+233 241 453 871 in Ghana
770 316 4217 in the U.S.
drsharita@yahoo.com

Newly Added Allopathic/Western Healthcare Providers

Dr. Tomicka Jackson-George,DMD, P.A.-Black Owned
Dentistry
www.jacksongeorgedental.com
410-685-2850

Dr.Frank P. Dawson, MD-Black Owned
Sports Medicine
www.medstarhealth.org/doctors/frank-prescott-dawson-iv-md 443 777-6788

Dr. Leonie M Prao, MD-Black Owned Sports Medicine https://www.medstarhealth.org/doctors/leonie-m-prao-md
410 554-6636

Dr. Dionne D. Oliver, MD-Black Owned
Gynecology/Obstetrics
Total Women's Health of Baltimore 443 471-3288
www.oliverobgyn.com/

Dr. Dana Truesdale, DDS-Black Owned
Dentistry
Innovation Dental Center
410-928-7696, (410) 383-7070

Dr. Michael Zollicoffer, MD-Black Owned
Pediatrician, Urgent Care 410-
542-1725

Dr.Joi L. Edwards, DMD-Black Owned
Dentistry
770-467-3888 /770-966-9396

Dr.Monique H. Golding, MD-Black Owned
Family Medicine Specialist 423-
892-2221

Dr. Kimberly M. Turner, MD-Black Owned
Obstetrics and Gynecology 443-
259-3770

Dr. Nadu Tuakli, MD, MPH -Black Owned
Family Medicine Specialist, Anti-Aging/Preventive Medicine www.anti-agingdoctor.com
410 992-0011

Dr. Earl Pearson-Black Owned
Dentist
215-242-1757

Dr. Kamau Kokayi -Black Owned Family Medicine
Holistic Medicine Specialist-Yale University School of Medicine 718-622-2042
https://healinghealthservices.com/

Dr. Benjamin Arthur, OD -Black Owned Perspective
Family Eyecare Optometrist 718-
708-5360
www.perspectiveyes.com

ALGERIA

ALGIERS

Annexe Cpmc - Black Friendly
Rue Freres Boudra

Cabinet de Rhumatologie, Dr A.Boukider - Black Owned, Black Friendly
53 Boulevard Des Martyrs Sidi M'Hamed

Cabinet Medical Dr Bakir Djamal - Black Owned, Black Friendly
48 Rue Oukil Hadj M'hamed logis postal Bt E -El-Mouradia

Dr.Yahiaoui Cabinet mÃ©dical et consultation Ã domicile - Black Friendly
CitÃ© 502 Logts Bt A9 n=â€¢1 hammamet Alger

Mushapa University Hospital Centre - Black Friendly
1945 Place du ler Mai Sidi M'Hamed

ANGOLA

HUAMBO

ClÃ-nica Chissola - Black Owned, Black Friendly
cidade baixa R Vicente Ferreira

Ervenaria Verdemental - Black Owned, Black Friendly
Huambo

International SOS Talatona Clinic - Black Owned,Black Friendly
Office Rua S10 Sector Talatona Zona CC-B2

LUANDA

Hospital Municipal da Samba - Black Owned, Black Friendly
Hospital Municipal da Samba

ClÃ-nica Sagrada EsperanÃ§a - Black Friendly
Av Murtala Mohammed

LUANDA MEDICAL CENTER - Black Owned, Black Friendly
R AmÃlcar Cabral 2b Luanda

ARGENTINA

BUENOS AIRES

Clinica de Ojos Dr. Nano San Miguel - Black Friendly
Domingo Faustino Sarmiento 1431 B1663 San Miguel Provincia de

Hospital Italiano de Buenos aires - Black Friendly
Peron 4190 CI199 ABH

Like Your Dentist - Black Friendly
Av Congreso 2174 C1428 CABA

AUSTRALIA

NSW - Sydney

My Doctors Medical Centre-Black Friendly
Shop 38 Glenquarie Tow n Centre Victoria Rd and Brooks St Macquarie Fields

St Vincent Hospital-Black Friendly
390 Victoria St Darlinghurst

Sydney Day Hospital-Black Friendly
1 187 Macquarie St VIC - Melbourne

Balanced Body Chiropractic-Black Owned,
Black Friendly 157 Scoresby Rd Boronia

Dr. Vadim Mirmilstein - Obstetrician and Gynecologist-Black Friendly
Suite 3 Level 3/182-184 Victoria Parade East Melbourne

The Integrated Medical Centre-Black Friendly
460 Brunswick St Fitzroy North VIC

AUSTRIA

WIEN-VIENNA

The Queen Elizabeth Hospital-Black Friendly
Bognergasse

Old Field Pharmacy-Black Friendly
Stephansplatz

Pharmacy of the Holy Spirit-Black Friendly
Operngasse

BAHARIN

MANAMA

Bahrain Pharmacy - Black Friendly
313 Bab Al Bahrain Ave

Good Life Pharmacy - Black Friendly
Road No 1911 Al Hoora building 339 Block 319

Juffair Pharmacy - Black Friendly
Strand Plaza FRONT OF CARIBOU COFFEE
Shop 491 1402 Shabab Ave

BANGLADESH

DHAKA

Al-Markazul Islami Hospital - Black Owned, Black Friendly
21 17 Babar Rd

Bangladesh Community General Hospital - Black Friendly
Demra Highway

Bangladesh Specialised Hospital - Black Friendly
Mirpur Road

BELGIUM

BRUSSELS

Pharmacie - Black Friendly
1000 Rue Montoyer 58 1000 Bruxelles Belgium

Pharmacie Lloydspharma Bruxelles Chartreux - Black Friendly
Rue des Fabriques 8 1000 Bruxelles Belgium

Uz Brussel - Black Owned
Avenue du laerbeek 101

BENIN

PORTO-NOVO

Clinique Louis Pasteur - Black Owned
Porto-Novo Benin

Pharmacie Agbokou - Black Owned,Black Friendly
Porto-Novo Benin

Pharmacie Tokpota-Davo - Black Owned,Black Friendly
Porto-Novo Benin

BOTSWANA

GABORNE

Afro Specialities - Black Friendly
Plot 14427Afro world center Kudumatse drive

Bokamoso Private Hospital - Black Friendly
Mmopane blk 1 plot 4769 0000 Gaborone Botswana

Botsogo Health Plan - Black Owned
Zambezi towers

BRAZIL

BRASILIA

Afetos Pediatria - Black Friendly
SGAS II St de Grandes Ã reas Sul 613 - Asa Sul Brasilia - DF 70200-001 Brazil

Dr Welber Sousa Oliveira - Black Friendly
SMHN QD 2 BL A (EdifÃcio de ClÃnicas - Salas 1001 e 1002 - Asa Norte Brasilia - DF 70710-904 Brazil

Drogaria Difor - Black Friendly
SHCS CLS 412 - Brasilia Federal District 70296-120 Brazil

RIO DE JANEIRO

Dr. Hilton Franco Pereira - Black Friendly
R AraÃºjo Porto Alegre 70 - Centro Rio de Janeiro - RJ 20030-012 Brazil

Drogarias Conceito - Black Friendly
PraÃ§a MauÃ¡ 17 - SaÃºde Rio de Janeiro - RJ 20081-240 Brazil

Farmacia de Manipula - Black Friendly
Av Henrique Dumont 65 - Ipanema Rio de Janeiro - RJ 22410-060 Brazil

SAO PAOLO

Acao Solidaria cantra o cancer infantil Ascci - Black Friendly
Oscar Freire 1990

Drugstore Sao Paulo - Black Friendly
Av Vital Brasil 1108 - ButantÃ£ SÃ£o Paulo - SP 05503-000 Brazil

Weleda do Brazil Ltda Laboratory and Pharmacy - Black Friendly
R JoÃ£o Cachoeira 112 - Itaim Bibi SÃ£o Paulo - SP 04535-010 Brazil

BULGARIA

SOFIA

Dr. Light Doshev - acupuncture, acupressure, manual therapy and natural medicine - Black Friendly
ul "Iskar" 40 1000 Sofia Center Sofia Bulgaria

Femina medical centre - Black Friendly
ul "Dunav" 47 1202 Sofia Center Sofia Bulgaria

Medical Center "Dr. Domusievi" - Black Friendly
ul "Bratya Miladinovi" 104-108 1000 Sofia Center Sofia Bulgaria

BURKINA FASO

OUAGADOUGOU

Clinique ALATAOU - Black Friendly
Koulouba Ouagadougou BurkinaFaso

Clinique Centre d'Or - Black Owned, Black Friendly
Patte dÂ´oie Ouagadougou Burkina Faso

Msf Ouaga - Black Owned, Black Friendly
Koulouba Ouagadougou Burkina Faso

BURUNDI

GITEGA

Health Center Sos - Black Friendly
Gitega Burundi

Hospital Regional De Gitega - Black Owned, Black Friendly
Hospital in Gitega Burundi

Clinical Vision Sante - Black Owned, Black
Friendly Gitega Burundi

CAMBODIA

PHNOM PENH

Marie Stopes International Cambodia - Black Friendly
Phnom Penh Centre Building F 1st Floor Sothearos BoulevardSangkat Tonle Bassac Khan Chamkarmorn 12301 Cambodia

Marie Stopes Takhmao Clinic - Black Friendly
No 538 St 201 Takhmao City Kandal 08251 Cambodia

Pha Phengan Dental Clinic - Black Owned,
Black Friendly Unnamed Road Phnom Penh Cambodia

CAMEROON

DOUALA

Dr Eric Meno - Black Friendly
Douala

Dr Josephine Mbuagbwa - Black Friendly
Douala

Dr M. Limagnack - Black Friendly
Douala

YAOUNDE

Dr Ngamy Elisabeth - Black Owned
Rue Frederic Foe Yaounde Cameroon

Dr Tankeo Medical Center - Black Owned
99054 Yaounde Cameroon

Pharmacie du soleil - Black Friendly
Avenue ahidjo

CANADA

MONTREAL

Katchoo Inc. - Black Owned, Black Friendly
6285 Rue de St-Vallier

Montreal General Hospital - Black Friendly
1650 Cedar Ave Montreal Quebec H3G 1A4 Canada

TORONTO

Dr Black Dola - Black Friendly
27 Roncesvalles Ave Toronto ON M6R 3B2 Canada

Dr. Alya Rahim MD - Black Friendly
790 Bay St #630 Toronto ON M5G 1N8 Canada

Sanomed Medical Walk-in & Family Clinic - Black Friendly
1000 Bay St unit A Toronto ON M5S 3A8 Canada

VANCOUVER

Sacred Circle Counselling - Black Owned,
Black Friendly 202-15388 24th Avenue South Surrey BC

Samantha Thoms RD - Black Owned, Black Friendly
900-2025 Willingdon Ave Burnaby BC V5C 0j3

CAPE VERDE PRAIA

ClÃnica MÃ©dico - DentÃ¡ria Caras & Bocas,lda. - Black Owned, Black Friendly R Uccla Praia Cape Verde

Dental ClÃnica - Black Owned, Black Friendly
Praia Cape Verde

Verdefam Sede - Black Owned, Black Friendly
Praia Cape Verde

CENTRAL AFRICAN REPUBLIC

BANGUI

GREEN WORLD - Black Owned
Bangui Central African Republic

Pharmacie communautaire - Black Owned
Bangui Central African Republic

Pharmacie du Centre Ville - Black Owned
Ctre Ville Central African Republic

CHAD

NDJAMENA

Clinique Vision Plus - Black Owned
N'Djamena Chad

International SOS Clinic - Black Owned
N'Djamena Chad

Wad Talb Centre OUWESS d'analyses medicales - Black Owned
N'Djamena Chad

CHILE

SANTIAGO

Farmacias Ahumada - Black Friendly
Av El Bosque Lota NÂ° 164 Santiago RegiÃ³n Metropolitana Chile

Knop pharmacies - Currency - Black Friendly
Moneda 1045 Santiago RegiÃ³n Metropolitana Chile

Pharmacies Knop - Alameda - Black Friendly
Av Libertador Bernardo O'Higgins 985 Santiago RegiÃ³n Metropolitana Chile

CHINA

BEIJING

Beijing hospital - Black Friendly
1dahua road

Dongchang PuRen hospital - Black Friendly
100 chong wen men outer St

Peking university first hospital - Black Friendly
8xishiku street

SHANGHAI

Huadong Hospital - Black Friendly
221 W Yan'an Road Jing'an District

Red House Hospital - Black Friendly
419 Fangxie Road in Huangpu District

Zhongshan Hospital - Black Friendly
Xuhui District

COLOMBIA

BOGOTA

Lafam Health clinics - Black Friendly
Ak 19 #151 - 75 BogotÃ¡ Colombia

Malo Clinic - Black Friendly
Cl 90 ##19a-29 BogotÃ¡ Colombia

Boston Medical Group - Black Friendly
Cra 10 #97A - 13 BogotÃ¡ Cundinamarca Colombia

CALI

Clinica Centri Imbanco - Black Friendly
Carrera 38 N 5A-100 cali

Clinica de accidente - Black Friendly
Calle 18 NRO 5 N34 cali

Drogueria Comfandi - Black Friendly
Colombia #5-281 Cali Valle del Cauca Colombia

MEDELLIN

Famicove - Black Friendly
Cl 57a ##48-55 MedellÃn Antioquia Colombia

Hospital General De MedellÃn Luz Castro De GutiÃ©rrez - Black Owned, Black Friendly
Cra 48 ###32 - 102 MedellÃn Antioquia Colombia

Pablo TobÃSn Uribe Hospital - Black Friendly
Calle 78b #NO 69 - 240 MedellÃn Antioquia Colombia COTE D'IVOIRE

ABIDJAN

Centre medical du Port Autonome d'Abidjan - Black Friendly
Boulevard de Vridi Abidjan Côte d'Ivoire

Dr Kouakou - Black Owned, Black Friendly
Plateau

SIÃGE DE L'ORDRE DES MEDECINS DE CÔTE D'IVOIRE– Black Friendly
Abidjan Côte d'Ivoire

CUBA

HAVANA

Centro de Histioterapia Placentaria - Black Friendly
1402 Calle 18 La Habana 10400 Cuba

ClÃnica Central Cira GarcÃa - Black Friendly
Ave Lazaro e/ 18 y 20 Pya La CÃ¡rdenas La Habana Cuba

PoliclÃnico Docente Martires del Corynthia - Black Friendly
Havana Cuba

SANTIAGO DE CUBA

Clinica Internacional Cubanacan - Black Friendly
Santiago de Cuba-Cuba

Hospital Clinico quirÃºrgico Ginecobstetrico - Black Friendly
Santiago de Cuba Cubde santiago de cuba-cuba

Hospital Materno Sur - Black Friendly
Avenida Victoriano de GarzÃ³n Santiago de Cuba-Cuba

CZECH REPUBLIC

PRAGUE

Dr.Max - Black Friendly
Na Po_Ã_Ã 30 110 00 NovÃ© M_sto Czechia

Farmacia LÃkÃ¡rna CÃsa_skÃ¡ - Black Friendly
Karlovo nÃ¡m 557 120 00 NovÃ© M_sto Czechia

LÃKÃRNA ipc Palladium - Black Friendly
NÃ¡m_stÃ Republiky 1078/1 110 00 NovÃ© M_sto Czechia

DEMOCRATIC REPUBLIC OF THE CONGO

KATANGA

Polyclinique Shalina - Black Owned, Black Friendly
Ave Patrice Emery Lumumba Lubumbashi Congo – Kinshasa

Dr Paul Maw aw - Black Ow ned, Black Friendly
148 Ave des Ecoles Lubumbashi Congo - Kinshasa

Medical Office Dr. Luty - Black Owned, Black Friendly
Avenue Lufira Lubumbashi Congo – Kinshasa

KISANGANI

Clinical Stanley - Black Owned
Kisangani Congo - Kinshasa

Cliniques Universitaires De Kisangani - Black Owned
Unnamed Road Kisangani Congo - Kinshasa

Hopital Du Cinquantenaire- Black Owned
Kisangani Congo – Kinshasa

DENMARK

COPENHAGEN

Citydoctors - Black Friendly
Lille StrandstrÃ¦de 20 1254 KÃ¸benhavn Denmark

Doctors.DK ApS - Black Friendly
Tuborg Parkvej 2 2900 Hellerup Denmark

Robert & Bolaji Balslev - Black Friendly
Ã˜sterbrogade 94 2100 KÃ¸benhavn Denmark

DJIBOUTI

DJIBOUTI

Djibouti Medical Center - Black Owned, Black Friendly
Djibouti Djibouti

Dr. Said Ali Douksiyeh - Black Owned, Black Friendly
Route de L'aÃ©roport Djibouti

SOM CLINIQUE ET CENTRE DE DIAGNOSTIC - Black Owned,
Black Friendly Rue de Athenes Djibouti

DOMINICAN REPUBLIC

PUNTA CANA

Dr Winston Santos Arismendy Plastic Surgery - Black Friendly
Edif Centur Blvd 1ro de Noviembre 403 Punta Cana 23000

Dominican Republic Hospiturs International Clinic del Este SRL - Black Friendly
Punta Cana 23000 Dominican Republic

Punta Cana Oral Health - Black Owned, Black Friendly
Edificio NÂ° 406 Cedro Punta Cana 23302 Dominican Republic

EGYPT

ALEXANDRIA

Hassab Hospital - Black Owned
92 Moharram Bek Em berouz WA Moharram Beik Moharam Bek
Alexandria Governorate Egypt

My Dental Clinic - Black Friendly
Home 5 Dr Ali Ibrahim Al Mesallah Sharq Al Attarin
Alexandria Governorate Egypt

Royal Clinic Specialty Clinics - Black Friendly
El-Samer Tower 40 Omar El-Mokhtar
Al Qasaei Bahri First Al Raml Alexandria Governorate Egypt

CAIRO

Dr Hassan ELHoshy - Black Owned
52 Abd El-Khalik Tharw at Madinet Al Eelam Agouza Giza Governorate Egypt

Dr Khaled Bahaaeldin Pediatric Surgery - Black Owned
2 Talaat Harb El-Zawya El-Hamraa Cairo Cairo Governorate 11451 Egypt

Dr.George Abdelfady Nashed. - Black Owned
11 Alfalaky square bab alluke downtown Cairo Cairo Governorate Egypt

EQUATORIAL GUINEA

MALABO

Clinica Cristisna - Black Friendly
Malabo Equatorial Guinea

Clinica Virgen De Guadalupe - Black Owned, Black Friendly
alle del Rey Malabo Malabo Equatorial Guinea

El Frio / Doctor Frio - Black Owned
558 Equatorial Guinea

ERITREA

ASMARA

Freedom Pharmacy - Black Owned, Black Friendly
Shegali St Asmara Eritrea

Halibet Hospital - Black Friendly
Asmara Eritrea

Orotta National Referral Hospital - Black Friendly
Aarerib St Asmara Eritrea

ETHIOPIA

ADDIS ABABA

Spectrum Laboratories PLC - Black Owned
Jommo Kenyatta

Dr. Mihretu Dermatology clinic - Black Friendly
Addis Ababa Ethiopia

Medecins Sans Frontieres (MSF) - Black Owned, Black Friendly
Addis Ababa Ethiopia

FRANCE

NICE

Dr Trojman Yves - Black Owned, Black Friendly
24 Rue de France 06000 Nice France

Dr. La Marca - Black Friendly
19 Rue de la LibertÃ© 06000 Nice France

Hospital prive Geriatrique les source - Black Owned
10 camin Rene pietruschi

PARIS

HÃ´pital EuropÃ©en Georges-Pompidou - Black Friendly
20 Rue Leblanc 75015 Paris France

Hospital Cochin - Black Friendly
27 Rue du Faubourg Saint-Jacques 75014 Paris France

Day hospital Gombault Darnaud - Black Owned
24 rue Bayen

GABON

LIBREVILLE

Centre Bien-Ãªtre Chinois - Black Friendly
Gabon Libreville AngondjÃ©

Pharmacie Charbonages - Black Owned, Black Friendly
Charbonnages Libreville Gabon

GAMBIA

BANJUL

BabuCarr Nyang - Black Owned
sinchu Sorri

Bakary - Black Owned, Black Friendly
Yundum

GERMANY

BERLIN

PGD International GmbH - Black Owned
Joachim friedrichdtraBe berlin

Dr. med. Nikolaus Peter HÃ¶llen - Black Friendly
KyffhÃ¤userstraÃŸe 11 10781 Berlin Germany

Martin Luther Hospital - Black Friendly
Caspar- TheyÃŸ-StraÃŸe 27-31 14193 Berlin Germany

MUNICH

M1 Private clinic AG - Black Owned
Frauenplatz 7

Klinikum Dritter orden-children's hospital - Black Owned
Menzinger str 44

Dr. Von Hauner Children's Hospital - Black Friendly
LindwurmstraBe 480337

GHANA

ACCRA

Nyaho medical center - Black Owned
35 Kofi Annan St Airport Residential Area Accra Ghana

37 Military Hospital - Black Owned, Black Friendly
Miils Rd Accra

Crown Medical Center - Black Owned
103 Hallelujah Broadway Adenta - Powerland Accra

KUMASI

Faith Maternity Home
PV Obeng Avenue

West End Hospital- Black Owned, Black Friendly
410 W End Hospital Bypass

ASAFO-BOAKYE SPECIALIST HOSPITAL- Black Owned
No 10 Asafo-Boakye street Ahenema Kokoben Kumasi

GREECE

ATHENS

Athens City Pharmacy- Black Friendly
Miaouli 6 & Themidos 1 Athina 105 54

Dr Pharmacy Omonoia- Black Friendly
Pl Omonias 19A Athina 104 31

mypharmacity.gr - Black Friendly
Lisimachias 24 AthensGreece 117 45

GUINEA

CONKRAY

CLINIQUE PASTEUR- Black Owned
5th boulevard

Hospital nationale Ignace Deen Black Friendly
6eme avenue koulewondy kaloum

Hospital Baptist - Black Owned
Vers le port Bonfi matam

GUINEA-BISSAU

BISSAU

Clinica madre Teresa de calcuta- Black Friendly
Avenida do brasil

Dr. Juan L. Sayu Stewart-Black Owned
Rua Angola no 9 Bissau

ORTODENTE - Black Owned
Rua Eduardo Mondlane

HAITI

PORT-AU-PRINCE

Dr.Pierre dental Clinic- Black Owned
118 ave Martin Luther king Port au Prince HT 1116

Partners In Development Medical Clinic-Black Owned
Port-au-Prince Haiti

Villa Sante- Black Owned
15 angle et rue Borno Petion-Ville Haiti Metellus Petion-Ville 6143

HUNGARY

BUDAPEST

Dr. Akos Santha (Neurology)- Black Friendl
Viranyos Klinika Viranyos ut 23/D

Dr. Balint Nemeth (Dentist)-Black Friendly
BL Dent Kft Kapas street 26-44 Building C

Dr. Felkai Peter (Anesthetics)- Black Friendly
Szentendrei ut 301

INDIA

BANGLORE

Aesthetics PLUS - Best Cosmetic & Plastic Surgery Clinic- Black Friendly
Suite 213 II Floor Eva Mall # 60 Brigade Road Above DECATHLON

Apollo Clinic-Black Friendly
769 1st Floor GYR Chambers Above Pai International Sarjapur Main Rd opp South Indian Bank

Dr. Banarji B H - Shoulder Specialis- Black Friendly
S3 4 8th Main Water Tank Rd CHBS Layout Vijayanagar

DAR ES SALAAM

GILDA PHARMACY- Black Friendly
CHANIKA TUNGINI

DELHI

All India Medicos- Black Friendly
Shop No 1 Meb Near AIIMS NDMC Market Yusuf Sarai

Guardian Pharmacy-Black Friendly
Plot No:18 Shop No: G- 4 & 5 Wadhwa Plaza 3 Mall Road Pocket 1 Sector 10 Below PNB Dwarka

Vandana Pharmacy - Shoulder Specialist- Black Friendly
Shop No 2 Surya Mansion 1 Kaushalya Park Chaudhary

MUMBAI

Dr Ishani Chakravarty@Aviva skin clinic- Black Friendly
Shop No 102 Powai Plaza 1st Floor
Adi Shankaracharya Marg Hiranandani Gardens Central Avenue Powai

Dr Mahima Jain Skin Hair Cosmetic and Laser Clinic-Black Friendly
12 Unity Heights Goregaon SV Rd Malad West Mumbai

My Skin My Health Clinic - Dr. Pallavi Rathi- Black Friendly
Unit No A 407/408 A Wing Saki Vihar Rd opp HP petrol pump Sag Baug Marol Saki Naka

INDONESIA

JAKARTA

Boston Drugs & Pharmacy Stores - Black Friendly
Cilandak Town Square Lt 1 Jl TB Simatupang Kav 17

Tropica Mas Pharmaceutical Indonesia - Black Friendly
Jakarta, Indonesia

IRELAND

DUBLIN

Blackrock Medical Clinic- Black Friendly
34 Main St Blackrock Co

Oakwood Medical Clinic, Castleknock - Black Friendly
1Castlecourt Shopping Centre 3

Weekend Doctor, Nassau Clinic - Black Friendly
32 Nassau Street Suite 17 on 1st Floor

ISRAEL

TEL AVIV

Dr. Kordevani Tel-Aviv Center Clinic- Black Friendly
Harav Reines St 18 Tel Aviv-Yafo

Tel Aviv Doctor - Black Friendly
Basel St 46 Tel Aviv-Yafo

Tel Aviv Medical Clinic - Black Friendly
Weizmann St 14 Tel Aviv-Yafo 6423914

ITALY

ROME

New clinic Annunzia tella- Black Owned
Via Meropia 124

Clinica mater Dei - Black Owned
Via Antonio Bertoloni

Clinia Ars Biomedical - Black Owned
Via luigi Bodio

FLORENCE

Farmacia Al PonteVecchio- Black Friendly
Lungarno degli Acciaiuoli 4r 50123Firenze

Farmacia Brizio - Mazzei- BlackFriendly
Via Ventisette Aprile 23 50129 Firenze

Uffizi Pharmacy - Black Owned
Via dei Neri 67/r 50122 Firenze

VENICE

Farmacia Al Castoro Dr. Aldo Navoni- Black Friendly
Ruga Vecchia S Giovanni 482 30125 Venezia

Farmacia Morelli - Mazzei- Black Friendly
Via Ventisette Aprile 23 50129 Firenze

Old Pharmacy In The World - The Speziere Of Venice - Black Owned
Sestiere de SMarco 1676 30124 Venezia

JAMAICA

KINGSTON

Access Medical Services- Black Owned
115 Hope Road Ligunaea Post Mall Unit # 14 Kingston 6

BBC Medical Services- Black Owned
Unit #2 Barbican Business Centre 88 Barbican Rd

Water Front Medical Centre - Black Owned
Shop 10 Office Center Building Ocean Blvd

JAPAN

HIROSHIMA

Chudenmae Pharmacy- Black Friendly
3 Chome-1-11 Otemachi Naka Ward Hiroshima 730-0051

BHIROSHIMA PREFECTUAL HOSPITAL- Black Friendly
1-5 54 UJINA-KANDAMINAMI-KU

SHIMA HOSPITAL - Black Friendly
NAKA-KU OOTEMACHI 1-5-25

OSAKA

Matsumoto Pharmacy- Black Friendly
2 Chome-3-18 Nakanoshima Kita Ward

Minami Pharmacy-Black Friendly
1 Chome-6-21 Ebisuhonmachi Naniwa Ward

Takeda Science Foundation (Osaka) - Black Friendly
3 Chome-1-2 Doshomachi Chuo Ward

TOKYO

PatFit- Black Friendly
2F Seiko Bldg 27-1 Sakuragaokacho Shibuya

The King Clinic-Black Friendly
Japan _150-0001 Tokyo Shibuya City Jingumae 6 Chome_31_11 iori B1F

Tokyo Medical And Surgical Clinic - Dr. Pallavi Rathi- Black Friendly Japan _105-0011 Tokyo Minato City Shibakoen 3 Chome_4_30 32 Nmf Shibakoen Building 2_

JORDAN

AMMAN

Drug Center Pharmacy - Black Friendly
Khalda_ Jordan

Drug Center Pharmacy Macca ST.- Black Friendly
Complex No 205 Mecca Al Mukarramah St 205 Amman

Jordan Hospital Pharmacy Alameda - Black Friendly
Jordan Hospital Adeeb Wahbeh St 25 Amman

KENYA

MOMBASA

Pandya Memorial Hospital - Black Owned
Dedan Kimathi Street

Pwani gyno centre - Black Friendly
SBM bank centre building Nyerere avenue

Meditrust health service - Black Friendly
80100 Bombolulu stage off nyali road NAIROBI

Aga Khan Hospital - Black Owned
Harambe avenue

Malibu pharmacy-Black Owned
Japan _150-0001 Tokyo Shibuya City Jingumae 6 Chome_31_11 iori B1F

NAIROBI WOMEN HOSPITAL- Black Owned
Kirichwa Road

LEBANON

BEIRUT

Cliniform Medical Aesthetics Clinic- Black Friendly
Tabaris Center 1603 Achrafieh Beirut

Dr. John Gebrane, Psychiatry - Black Friendly
Clemenceau Medical Center_ 5th Floor New Clinics Building_ Beirut

MIND Clinics - Black Friendly
Hamra Maamari Street Specialty Clinics Building_ Beirut

LESOTHO

MASERU

Faith Women's Clinic - Black Friendly
Dedan Kimathi Street

Karabo Family Clinic - Black Owned
Maseru Lesotho

Lehlakeng Clinic- Black Friendly
Cnr Airport Rd & Moshoeshoe Rd Maseru Lesotho

LIBERIA

MONROVIA

Redemption Hospital - Black Owned
New Kru Town

Snapper Hill Clinic - Black Owned
20 Roberts St

Albertine's Health Center- Black Owned
New Georgia Bassa Town Road Block"C"

LIBYA

TRIPOLI

Albaraa Hospital - Black Friendly
Jamaa Assaqaa Rd Tripoli Libya

Burns and Cosmetic Hospital - Black Friendly
Tripoli Libya

Tripoli Central Hospital - Black Friendly
Az Zawiyah St Tripoli Libya

MADAGASCAR

ANTANANARIVO

Assistance+ - Black Owned
Villa First Mandrosoa Ivato Lot 441ME Andafiavaratra Tanambao

Modern Medical Mihary Soa - Black Owned
Lot II R 31 Betongolo Rue Foloalindahy Malagasy Antananarivo

Rafarence Madicale- Black Owned
Jean Andriamady Rd Antananarivo

MALAWI

LILONGWE

Kamuzu central hospital - Black Owned Mzimba road area 33 Kachere Clinic - Black Owned Area 23 Kachere

Mars Hospital- Black Owned
Along Old 43 Road Area 10

MALAYSIA

KUALA LUMPUR

Chiropractic Specialty Center Sdn. Bhd.- Black Friendly
Plaza Damansara No 19 Jalan Medan Setia 1 Bukit Damansara 50490

Clique Clinic Bangsar - Black Friendly
6th floor Boutique Office 3A-06-01 Menara 3A 3 Jalan Bangsar Kampung Haji Abdullah Hukum 59200

Clique Clinic PJ- Black Friendly
No 4 Jalan 19/36 Seksyen 19 46300 Petaling Jaya Selangor

MALI

BAMAKO

Medical Mali.- Black Owned
Unnamed Road Bamako Mali

Medical Center "Happiness"- Black Owned
Unnamed Road Bamako Mali

Polyclinique Guindo- Black Owned
Rue 18 porte 19 Badala-Est BP E2267

MAURITANIA

NOUAKCHOTT

Cabinet Sahel Medical- Black Owned
Unnamed Road Nouakchott Mauritania

Clinique Chourouk d'ophtalmologie- Black Owned
Unnamed Road Nouakchott Mauritania

Clinique Elyousser- Black Owned
Avenue Moktar Ould Daddah

MAURITIUS

PORT LOUIS

City Clinic- Black Owned
Sir Edgar Laurent St

Dr M. N. Jahn Medical Centre- Black Owned
Rue Ashary

The Eye Clinic - Home of The Retinologist- Black Owned
22 Enniskillen St

MEXICO

GUADALAJARA

Antonio Diaz Bringas- Black Friendly
Av Mexico 2385 Ladron de Guevara Ladron De Guevara 44600

Doctor Jesus Octavio Navarro Grano Cirugia Ortopedica de Minima Invasion-Black Friendly
Calle Cruz Verde 73 Zona Centro 44100

DR. JORGE ECHEAGARAY HERRERA- Black Friendly
Calle Tarascos 3473 Monraz 44670

MEXICO CITY

Hospital De Jesus - Black Friendly
Av 20 de Noviembre 82 Centro Historico de la Ciudad de Mexico

Dr. Enrique Cabrera General Hospital- Black Friendly
Prol 5 de Mayo 3170 Ex hacienda de Tarango Alvaro Obregon 01620

Hospital Shriners Mexico- Black Friendly
Av del Iman No257 Pedregal de Santa Ursula Deleg Coyoaco¡n 09820

TIJUNA

Farmacia Discont Pharmacy - Black Friendly
Av Revolucion 615 Centro 22000

Gusher Farmacia Plaza Rio Tijuana - Black Friendly
Av Paseo de los Horoes 9550 Zona Urbana Rio Tijuana 22010

Tj Pharmacy- Black Friendly
Av Revolucion 911 Centro 22000

MOROCCO

CASABLANCA

Cabinet Medical Dr.Yahya Idrissi - Black Owned
64 boulevard Hassan El Alaoui 1er Etage Appart N2Ain Borja

CENTRE MEDICAL AUSTRALIEN- Black Owned
8 ghandi mall Casablanca -Maroc_ Boulevard Ghandi

Clinical Val D'anfa - Black Owned
Boulevard Franklin Roosevelt

MARRAKECH

Cabinet DR RAZIK - Black Friendly
Rue el Iraq

Dr Kaoutar El Benna-Ghidalia- Black Friendly
1 avenue Mohamed 6

Dr. Med Gertrud Michaelis- Black Friendly
7 Rue Ibn Sina

RABAT

Cabinet Dr. Zrarqi - Black Owned
1er Etage No11 Rue Al Mamouniya Immeuble 10

Clinique Slaoui de Chirurgie Esthetique Maroc - Black Owned
242 R401 Rabat 10170

Dr Elouakili Traumatologue Orthopodiste- Black Owned
54 angle avenue Oqbaa et rue ain asserdoun apt 8 agdal

MOZAMBIQUE

MAPUTO

Clinica Cruz Azul- Black Owned
Av Karl Marx 414 1

Clinica Vida Plena Lda - Black Owned
Av 25 Setembro 916

Maputo Private Hospital - Black Owned
Rio Inhamiara Road Sommerschield II

MYANMAR

YANGON

AUNG YADANA HOSPITAL- Black Owned
16 2 WARDTHIRIGON HOUSING

Myittar Mon Pharmacy - Black Friendly
141 143 Anaw rahta Rd Corner of Lanmadaw St and Ward (7) Anaw rahta Rd

PUN HLAING SILOAM HOSPITAL - Black Friendly
3 SHUNKHINTHAR Rd

NAMIBIA

WINDHOEK

Dr Desmond Uahungira Kandjoze Dentist- Black Owned
Shop 6 Independence Shopping Centre Independence Avenue Katutura

Erongo Med - Black Owned
6th copper

Shaetonjodhi Optics - Black Owned
Independence Avenue

NETHERLANDS

AMSTERDAM

Academic Medical Centre- Black Owned
Merbergdree

Helder kliniek Amsterdam- Black Owned
Laardehoogtweg

Amsterdam Central Pharmacy - Black Friendly
De Ruijterkade 24a 1012 AA

NEW ZEALAND

AUCKLAND

The Travel Doctor- Black Friendly
170 Queen Street Auckland CBD

Eastmed Doctors - Black Friendly
188 Saint Heliers Bay Road St Heliers

Lovrich Black & Van Der Steeg - Black Friendly
Cnr Beach & Anzac Roads Brow ns Bay

NIGER

NIAMEY

Clinique de La Paix - Black Owned
Avenue de Djermakoye

Clinique Olivia - Black Owned
Unnamed Road Niger

Medical Office Tayamana - Black Owned
Niamey Niger

NIGERIA

ABUJA

Kelina Medical Centre- Black Owned
116 3rd Avenue Gwarimpa

Bridge clinic - Black Owned
Gwaska street

Nisa Premier Hospital - Black Owned
15 21 Alex Ekwueme Way Jabi

KANO

Almu Memorial Hospital - Black Owned
Maiduguri Road Tarauni

Barewa Clinic - Black Owned
Zaria Road

Hasiya Bayero Pediatric hospital- Black Owned
Emir Palace Rd Kofar Dan Agudi

LAGOS

Alpha Pharmacy & Stores - Black Owned
33 Adeniyi Jones Ave Oba Akran Ikeja

Dannis Ashley Wellness Center - Black Owned
Oniru estate Victoria island

St Nicholas Hospital- BlackOwned
St Nicholas Hospital Lagos Island

PAKISTAN

KARACHI

MedicalStore.com.pk- Black Friendly
Online Pharmacy in Pakistan

Ali Chemist & Pharmacy - Black Friendly
38 A 10th Street beside Dha clinics Khayaban-e-Rahat DHA Phase 6

Health Mart Pharmacy - Black Friendly
9 1 33-A St Block 4 Clifton

PANAMA

PANAMA CITY

American Medical Centers - Friendly
Brazilian Beauty Valaq ViaEspaia Panama City Panama

Dr. Luis Picard-Ami, Jr. - Black Friendly
Avenida Central Espaia

Panama Chiropractic Health Center- Black Friendly
Plaza Balboa Local 10 Nivel 2 Cinta Costera

PERU

LIMA

Boticas Ahorro Y Farma- Black Friendly
Antofagasta 2000 Cercado de Lima

Boticas Delta Farma - Black Friendly
Gardenias Cercado de Lima

Farmamia Benavides - Black Friendly
Av Alfredo Benavides 2220-2298 Cercado de Lima

POLAND

WARSAW

Apteka przy Placu Zbawiciela - Black Friendly
Mokotowska 12 00-640

Independent Public Central Clinical Hospital - Black Friendly
UlBanacha 1a

Prosektorium kasprzaka szpital wolski-Black Friendly
Ulkasprzaka

PORTUGAL

LISBON

Farmacia Andrade - Black Friendly
R do Alecrim 125 127 1200-016 Lisboa

Medical One - Centro Clinico- Black Friendly
R Adriano Correia de Oliveira 6 1600-312 Lisboa

Farmajcia Estajcio - Black Friendly
Prasa dos Restauradores 15 1250-187 Lisboa

PUERTO RICO

SAN JUAN

Walgreens Pharmacy - Black Friendly
700 Avenida Roberto H Todd

First Pharmacy - Black Friendly
670 Avenida de la Constitucion

QATAR

DOHA

Family Medicine Specialists in Qatar - Black Friendly
Al Waab St

Royal Medical Center - Black Friendly
Al Muntazah street Nuaija area Al Hilal West Doha

ROMANIA

BUCHAREST

Farmacia Academia - Black Friendly
Strada Academiei 35-38 Bucure_ti 030167

Farmacia Sandoria - Black Friendly
Sos Viilor 78-88 Bucuresti-Sector 5 Bucuresti 50157

Farmacie APIFARM- Black Friendly
Strada C A Rosetti 35-27 Bucure_ti 030167

RUSSIA

ST. PETERSBURG

clinic Scandinavia - Black Friendly Ulitsa Il'yushina 4/1

Lakhta Klinika Na Savushkina - Black Owned
Ulitsa Savushkina 73/50 St Petersburg Leningrad Oblast

North-Western State Medical University - Black Friendly
Kirochnaya Ulitsa 41

RWANDA

KIGALI

Inkuru Nziza Hospital - Black Owned
KK 565 St

La Croix du Sud Hospital - Black Owned
KG 201 St

Polyclinique LA MEDICALE - Black Owned
KN 3 Rd Kigali Place Saint Paul

SAO TOME

SAO TOME

Farmacia Cabral - Black Friendly
Av da Independencia

Hospital Ayres de Menezes - Black Friendly
Bairro do hospital

Farmacia Epifanio- Black Friendly
Rua de Angola

SAUDI ARABIA

RIYADH

Diamond Shine Clinics - Black Friendly
Strada Academiei 35-38 Bucure_ti 030167

Diamond Shine Clinics - Black Friendly
Strada Academiei 35-38 Bucure_ti 030167

Magrabi Eye & Dental Center - Ghernata - Black Friendly
Eastern Ring Rd Ghirnatah

The Clinics- Black Friendly
Prince Muhammad Bin Abdulaziz Rd Al Olaya

SENEGAL

DAKAR

Cabinet Medical du Dr. Ibrahim Badaoui - Partenaire AfriDoctor - Black Owned
38 Rue Amadou Assane Ndoye

Clinique Cheikh Anta Diop - Dr Nafissatou Ndoye - Partenaire Afridoctor Black Owned
Avenue Cheikh Anta Diop

SEYCHELLES

VICTORIA

Dr Chetty's Medical Centre - Black Friendly
Malakoff St

Le Chantier Health Services - Black Friendly
Jivan's Complex Mahe

SIERRA LEONE

FREETOWN

Ahmadiyya Hospital - Black Owned
Hanga Road Kenema

Abanita Pharmaceutical - Black Owned
23 Ecowas St

Davidson Nicol Medical Center - Black Owned
3 Bright Lane Cole Farm off Wilkinson Rd

SINGAPORE

SINGAPORE

Central 24-HR Clinic (Woodlands) - Black Friendly
768 Woodlands Ave 6 #02-06A

National Skin Centre - Black Friendly
1 Mandalay Rd

Raffles Women Centre - Black Friendly
585 N Bridge Rd Level 12 Raffles Hospital

SOMALIA

MOGADISHU

Bukaan-Caawiye Medical Clinic - Black Owned
Wadada Cirtoogte

Somali Sudanese Specialized Hospital (SSSH)- Black Owned
Hodan Mogadishu BN

SKY Clinic- Black Owned
Makkah Almukarramah Ave

SOUTH AFRICA

CAPE TOWN

Iyeza Health- Black Owned
Unit 14 Prodev Park 2 Aviation Crescent Airport City

Dr P Mdletshe- Black Owned
Ubuntu Medical Centre 75 Dieperink St Roodepoort 1724

Kawena Better Life - Black Owned
Sunshine Plaza

JOHANNESBURG

Black Chain Pharmacy - Black Owned
Chris Hani Road 2001

Dr Maphisa& Partners incorporated - Black Owned
10th Floor Room 1010 Lister Building195 Rahima Moosa Street CBD

Genesis Maternity Clinic - Black Owned
5 Northwold Dr 2132

SOUTH KOREA

SEOUL

Korea University Medical Center - Black Friendly
73 Inchon-ro Anam-dong Seongbuk-gu

Korean Red Cross Hospital - Black Friendly
9 Saemunan-ro Gyonam-dong Jongno-gu

Sahmyook Medical Center - Black Friendly
82 Mangu-ro Hwigyeong 1(il)-dong Dongdaemun-gu

SOUTH SUDAN

JUBA

EB Clinic - Black Owned
768 Woodlands Ave 6 #02-06A

Juba Medical Complex - Black Owned
Unity road
Morobu Clinic - Black Owned
National Security Road

SPAIN

BARCELONA

European University hospital Alliance - Black Friendly
Passeig de la Vall d' Hebron

Farmacia Nadal- Black Friendly
La Rambla 121 08002

Vall d' Hebron Unversity Hospital - Black Friendly
Passeig de la Vall d' Hebron

MADRID

Hospital Infantil Unversitario Nino Jesus - Black Friendly
vde Menendeze Pelayo

MD Anderson Cancer Center Madrid - Black Friendly
Arturo Soria Street

San Camilo Hospital - Black Friendly
Calle de Juan Bravo

SRI LANKA

COLOMBO

Kirulapone Medical Centre - Black Friendly
165 1a Sri Siddhartha Rd

MyDoctor.lk - Black Friendly
Muhandiram E D Dabare Rd

Norris Clinic - Black Friendly
49 Norris Canal Rd Colombo 01000

SWEDEN

STOCKHOLM

Stockholm Heart Center AB - Black Owned
Kungsgatan 34

Medical Doctor Tiina Ahonen - Black Friendly
Fleminggatan 65 112 32

Urban OM (yoga and meditation)- Black Owned
Wallingatan 20-23

TAIWAN

TAIPEI CITY

SGreat Tree Pharmacy - Black Friendly
No 400 Section 2 Bade Road Songshan District

Yes Chain Pharmacy - Black Friendly
No 10 Section 3 Heping East Road Daean District Taipei City

TANZANIA

DAR ESSALAAM

Jabu Health Foundation - Black Owned
Chimera Street

Dr Paul Masua - Black Owned
Kinondoni

Aljumaa Charitable Dispensary - Black Owned
Sikukuu Street

THAILAND

BANGKOK

Dr Donna Robinson - Black Friendly
Floor 3 Building 2 of The Racquet Club Sukhumvit 49/9 Alley 10110

First Fertility PGS Center Bangkok - Black Friendly Unit A8-I88th Floor Golden Land Building Mahardlekluang 1 Lumphini Pathum Wan District

NICHE Natural Health- Black Friendly MedAsia Healthcare Complex Floor 9 14/9 Soi Sukhumvit 5 Klong Toei Nuea Watthana

TUNISIA

TUNIS

Centre Montfleury Medical- Black Owned
13 Ave Taha Hussein

Dr.Ben Hassen Aymen - Black Owned
102 Avenue Hedi Saidi Bab Saadoun Tunis in front of station metro T

Gynaecologist Dr Ahmed SKHIRI- Black Owned
Le triangle Medical 5 avenue Habib Bourguiba Le Bardo

TURKEY

ANKARA

Bensen Pharmacy - Black Friendly
Kelay Mh zmir-1 Cd 11/B 06420 Ankaya/Ankara

D_LEK SIHHIYE ECZANES_ - Black Friendly
Sa_iak mahallesi AAdnan Saygun Cd No:6 D:3 06600 Ankaya

Sever Pharmacy- Black Friendly
Ankaya Maltepe Mahallesi Onur Sokak No:38 Vehbi Koasa–_renci Yurdu arkasa 06570

UGANDA

KAMPALA

Nakasero hospital- Black Owned
Nakasero Hill Road

Case Medical Centre - Black Owned
69-71 Buganda Rd

Ecopharm Pharmacy Uganda Limited- Black Owned
Ntinda Rd

UKRAINE

KIEV

Kaplya Rosy Black Friendly
Sribnokilska St 20 Kyiv

Pharmacy # 1 - Black Friendly
Velyka Zhytomyrska St 8/14 Kyiv

Pharmacy Good Day- Black Friendly
107 Saksahanskoho St Kyiv

UNITED ARAB EMIRATES

ABU DHABI

Cleveland Clinic Abu Dhabi- Black Friendly
Zayed The First St - Jazeerat Al MaryahSowwah Square

CosmeSurge - Bareen International Hospital - Black Friendly
City Zone 15 next to Shaikah Fatima Bint Mubarak Mosque

CosmeSurge - Khalifa City A- Black Friendly
Corner of street 16 and 33 near Khalifa A Post Office

DUBAI

Aga Khan University Hospital- Friendly Office # 514 5th Floor Oud Metha Offices Complex Oud Metha Road Umm Hureir 2

American Hospital Media City Clinic - Black Friendly
Business Central Towers - Al SufouhAl Sufouh 2

Mediclinic Al Qusais - Black Friendly
#4 Ground Floor Dubai Residential OasisDamascus Street Al Qusais

UNITED KINGDOM

GLASLOW

NUFFIELD HEALTH GLASGOW HOSPITAL- Black Friendly
25 BEACONSFIELD Rd

BMI ROSS HALL HOSPITAL - Black Friendly
221 CROOKSTON Rd

Drs Leslie and Partners- Black Friendly
Woodside Health & Care Centre 891 Garscube Rd

LONDON

Joy's Health Sanctuary - Black Owned
29 Winslade Way

Royal Free Hospital - Black Friendly
Pond St Hampstead London NW3 2QG UK

University College Hospital- Black Friendly
235 NW Euston Rd Bloomsbury

UNITED STATES

ALASKA - ANCHORAGE

Walgreens Pharmacy - Black Friendly
725 E Northern Lights Blvd

Bernie's Pharmacy- Black Friendly
4100 Lake Otis Pkwy #200

Great Land Infusion Pharmacy - Black Friendly
2421 E Tudor Rd #107

ARIZONA - PHOENIX

Black, Kelly J MD- Black Friendly
4530 N 32nd St #100

David Black, O.D. - Black Friendly
1831 E Camelback Rd B2

Dr. Delbert R. Black, MD- Black Friendly
1850 N Central Ave # 1600

CALIFORNIA - LOS ANGELES

Cedars Sinai Medical Centre- Black Friendly
Los Angeles, CA

Good Samaritan hospital - Black Friendly
1225 Wilshire Blvd

Jeanette Black, MD- Black Friendly
9201 Sunset Blvd #602

COLORADO - DENVER

ClearSpring Pharmacy - Cherry Creek- Black Owned
201 University Blvd

The Centre For African American Health - Black Friendly
3350 Hudson St

Denver Health Pharmacy - Black Friendly
301 W 6th Ave Fl 1

DISTRICT OF COLUMBIA - WASHINGTON

Center for Dermatology and Dermatologic Surgery - Black Owned
725 E Northern Lights Blvd

Howard University Hospital- Black Owned
2041 NW Georgia Ave

Eye Doctors of Washington - Black Friendly
Lower 1016 16th St NW Level 100

FLORIDA - MIAMI

Florida Health Miami Dade County,
Test Miami testing center- Black Friendly
2515 W Flagler St

Little Haiti Health Center - Black Owned
300 NE 80th Terrace

South Regional Health Center- Black Friendly
4105 Pembroke Rd

FLORIDA - ORLANDO

Dr Andrea Black P.A.- Black Friendly
200 Ernestine St

Dr. Rafael E. Pinero, MD - Black Owned
1720 S Orange Ave #200

Pure Skin Dermatology & Aesthetics- Black Owned
10727 Narcoossee Rd B6

CHICAGO - ILLINOIS

2020 Organics- Black Owned
1448 E 52nd St

Premiere Health Urgent Care - Black Owned
1301E 47th Street Chicago

Provident Hospital of Cook County - Black Owned
500 E 51st St

INDIANA – INDIANAPOLIS

Doctors Skin Care - Dermatologist:Obeime Chris MD OD FAAD- Black Owned
8330 Naab Rd # 315

Aesculapian Medical Society - Black Friendly
222 E 63rd St

David J. Black, M.D. Gastroenterologist- Black Friendly
8325 S Emerson Ave suite b-1

MASSACHUSETTS - BOSTON

Black Mental Health Alliance of Massachusetts- Black Friendly
15 Drummond St

Peter Black MD - Black Friendly
44 Binney St

Richard Black MD - Black Friendly
340 Wood Rd #305

MICHIGAN - DETROIT

Detroit Receiving Hospital - Black Friendly
4201 St Antoine

Health and Wellness Store- Black Friendly
16140 W 7 Mile Road

Hutzel Women's Health Specialists - Black Friendly
4727 St Antoine #304

NORTH CAROLINA - CHARLOTTE

Dr. Mala A. Freeman-Kwaku, MD- Black Owned
3125 Springbank Ln # B

Your Wellness Key - Black Owned
3010 Monroe Road Suite 101

Dr. Steven L Gilchrist, MD- Black Owned
13425 Hoover Creek Blvd

NEVADA - LAS VEGAS

Couture Medical - Black Friendly
2615 Box Canyon Dr

Family Doctors Of Green Valley - Black Friendly
2626 S Rainbow Blvd

Scarff J Michael MD - Black Friendly
1934 E Sahara Ave

OHIO - CLEVELAND

The Black Mental Health Corp.- Black Friendly
13110 Shaker Square suite c200

Cosmopolitan Dermatology - Black Owned
2323 Lee Rd Cleveland Heights

Dr. Denise S. Black - Black Owned
2500 Metrohealth Dr

OREGON - PORTLAND

Dr.Marcelitte Failla, Chiropratic Physician- Black Owned
Portland, OR

AFC Urgent Care NW Portland - Black Friendly
25 NW 23rd Pl

Providence Portland Medical Center: Department of Hospitalist - Black Friendly
4805 NE Glisan St

PENNSYLVANIA - PHILADELPHIA

Dr. Paul's Holistic Health Network- Black Owned
501 King St

Susan Taylor MD - Black Owned
932 Pine St

(Gynecologist) Today's Woman:
Sharan Abdul-Rahman, MD, MBA, NCMP - Black Friendly
1015 Chestnut St #907

TEXAS - HOUSTON

Camille Cash, M.D.- Black Owned
2150 Richmond Ave #103

Irby Jones Edith MD - Black Owned
2601 Prospect St

Kemba Black, MD, FAAP - Black Owned
13105 Wortham Center D

VIRGINIA - NORFOLK

Community Personal Care, Inc.- Black Owned
1761 Church St

Brian Johnson MD - Black Friendly
5630 Lowery Rd

Northfolk Community Hospital - Black Friendly
600 Gresham Drive

VIRGINIA - RICHMOND

Walgreens Pharmacy- Black Friendly
1169 N Military Hwy

Bremo Pharmacy - Black Friendly
2024 Staples Mill Rd

Erin Reese MD - Black Friendly
401 N 11th St

VIETNAM

HANOI

Nguyen Luan Pharmacy- Black Friendly
3 Trang Thi Trang Tion Hoan Kiom HaNoi

Pharmacies France Vietnam - Black Friendly
E2 S 117 Phong Mai ong oa HaNoi

ZAMBIA

LUSAKA

Lusaka Trust Hospital - Black Owned
Plot 2190 Nsumbu rd woodlands

Bwafwano Community Health Clinic - Black Owned
Kabanana Road

Dr. Agarwal's Eye Hospital - Black Owned
Stand 599 Protea Road Opp Fairview Hotel / Off Church Rd

ZIMBABWE

HARARE

Divine Pharmacy - Black Owned
Fife Avenue Shopping Centre Shop No1 Athenitis Fifth Street

New Cranborne Maternity - Black Owned
Cranborne Harare

Westend Medical Center - Black Owned
3708 2nd street kuwadzana 2

Chapter 2: Holistic Health and Wellness

This special edition Global Green Book will focus on Holistic healing and the various paths/approaches to creating wellness. We will offer explanations of some common holistic healing modalities and explore the principles of holistic healing. Some modalities will be highlighted along with some renowned healers. In addition to the holistic therapies, we have included some additional life-saving information (signs of stroke, heart attack, toxicity, symptoms of diabetes and hypertension). We have also added to the first addition, a list of practitioners that specialize in holistic wellness. We are focusing on the health category first because we understand that without the optimal health of our people, we will not be able to fight for the eradication of racism and xenophobia. We wish to empower Black people with the knowledge to gain, re-gain and maintain supreme health in the body, mind, and spirit. The gathered information is this guide along with the directory of practitioners and healers is our way of healing Black people around theglobe.

Holistic wellness is an approach to being healthy that looks at a person's health in a holistic way. This considers their body, mind, and spirit. Attention to all three is needed to stay balanced and obtain optimal health and wellness. There are many terms that are used interchangeably to describe modalities that take a holistic approach to promote healing. They include, but are not limited to Alternative Medicine, Holistic Medicine, Complementary and Alternative Medicine,Mind-Body Medicine, Folk Medicine and Traditional Healing.

Holistic Healing Principles

1. Optimal Health is the primary goal of holistic medical practice. It is the conscious pursuit of the highest level of functioning and balance of the physical, environmental, mental, emotional, social, and spiritual aspects of human experience, resulting in a dynamic state of being fully alive. This creates a condition of well-being regardless of the presence or absence of disease.
2. The Healing Power of Love. Holistic healthcare practitioners strive to meet the patient with grace, kindness, acceptance, and spirit without condition, as love is life's most powerful healer.
3. Whole Person. Holistic healthcare practitioners view people as the unity of body, mind, spirit, and the systems in which theylive.
4. Prevention and Treatment. Holistic healthcare practitioners promote health, prevent illness, and help raise awareness of dis-ease in our lives rather than merely managing symptoms. A holistic approach relieves symptoms, modifies contributing factors, and enhances the patient's life system to optimize future well-being.
5. Innate Healing Power. All people have innate powers of healing in their bodies, minds, and spirits. Holistic health care practitioners evoke and help patients utilize these powers to affect the healing process.
6. Integration of Healing Systems. Holistic healthcare practitioners embrace a lifetime of learning about all safe and effective options in diagnosis and treatment. These options come from a variety of traditions and are selected in order to best meet the unique needs of the patient. The realm of choices may include
7. lifestyle modification and complementary approaches as well as conventional drug and surgery.
8. Relationship-centered Care. The ideal practitioner-patient relationship is a partnership which encourages patient autonomy and values the needs and insights of both parties. The quality of this relationship is an essential contributor to the healing process.

9. Individuality. Holistic healthcare practitioners focus patient care on the unique needs and nature of the person who has an illness rather than the illness that has the person.
10. Teaching by Example. Holistic healthcare practitioners continually work toward the personal incorporation of the principles of holistic health, which then profoundly influence the quality of the healingrelationship.
11. Learning Opportunities. All life experiences including birth, joy, suffering and the dying process are profound learning opportunities for both patients and healthcare practitioners.

These principles embraced by the Members of the Academy of Integrative Health and Medicine

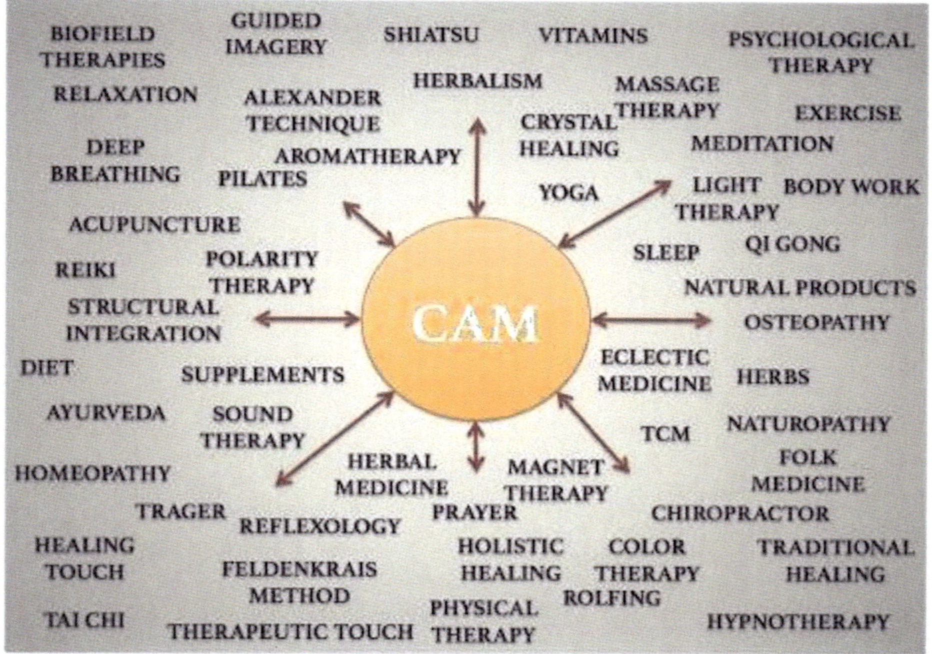

This chart illustrates the various healing modalities under the “Complementary and Alternative Medicine” model.

TYPES OF HOLISTIC TREATMENTS

ACUPUNCTURE

Conventional Chinese Medicine Acupuncture is done through the insertion of very thin needles into particular points on the body by a trained acupuncturist.

AROMATHERAPY

Inhaling fragrance of essential oils Aroma therapy involves inhaling the fragrance of essential oils extracted from particular plants. such as rosemary a lavender.

AYURVEDIC HEALING

Ayurveda Ayurvedic Healing is based that the human body is made up of a mixture of air. water. earth. fire. and space which combine to form 3 doshas (Vata. Kapha, and Pitta)

CHIROPRACTIC

AMA Chiropractors Chiropractors are designated by the AMA as physician-level providers who focus on disorders of the nervous system and musculoskeletal system.

DIETARY SUPPLEMENTS

Dietary Supplement - Holistic Way Dietary Supplements are used as a part of the holistic approach and are included in healing protocols used by holistic doctors, naturopathic doctors. and functional medicine doctors.

Herbal Aides: Nature's Healing Herbals

Compiled by Nana Akua Zenzele, Traditional Healer

"God made the earth yield healing herbs which the prudent man should not neglect." Ecclesiastes 38:4

Herbal Medicine is defined as the medicinal use of herb plants and trees to regain and/or maintain health. Herbs can be used to cleanse, detoxify, rebuild, and tone to bring the body back into balance. Mother nature should be appreciated not only for her beauty but also for her valuable resource of wild foods and medicines. These wonderful cures from the earth are often neglected and under-rated. There are herbal remedies for nearly every dis-ease or illness known to man. Herbs were commonly used before western pharmaceuticals were introduced and are still used today for regaining and maintaining the body, mind, and spirit's balance. Herbs may be used in the form of teas, capsules, tinctures, and various topicals. Below are some common easy-to-find/make herbals to have on hand for common everyday health complaints.

Ginger cleanses the colon, reduces spasms and cramps, and stimulates circulation; a strong antioxidant and effective antimicrobial agent for sores and wounds; useful for bowel disorders, circulatory problems, fever, hot flashes, indigestion, morning sickness, motion sickness, nausea, and vomiting. Can be used in the form of tea, tincture/extract, or capsules.

Valerian improves circulation and acts as a sedative; reduces mucus from colds; good for anxiety, fatigue, high blood pressure, insomnia, irritable bowel syndrome, menstrual cramps, muscle cramps, nervousness, pain, spasms, stress, and ulcers. Can be used in capsule or tincture/extract form. May also be used in tea, but the taste is a bit unpleasant so mixing with other nervine or sedative herbs would be advisable.

Cayenne aids digestion, improves circulation, and stops bleeding from ulcers; good for heart, kidneys, lungs, pancreas, spleen, and stomach; useful for arthritis and rheumatism; helps ward off colds, sinus infections, and sore throats. Use in capsule form. Good for pain when applied topically.

Garlic detoxifies the body and protects against infection by enhancing immune function; lowers blood pressure and improves circulation; aids in the treatment of arteriosclerosis, arthritis, asthma, cancer, circulatory problems, colds and flu, digestive problems, heart disorders, insomnia, liver disease, sinusitis, ulcers, and yeast infections; good for virtually and any disease or infection. Can be used in raw, fresh form or taken in odor-less tablet form for more adequate, consistent supply.

Rosemary fights bacteria, relaxes the stomach, stimulates circulation and digestion, and acts as astringent and decongestant, good for headaches, high and low blood pressure, circulatory problems, and menstrual cramps. Can be used in the forms of tea or capsules.

Charcoal removes toxic substances from the colon and bloodstream; useful for gas, upset stomach, food poisoning, and diarrhea; and antidote for nearly all poisons. Can be taken in the form of powder or capsules/tablets. 27

Aloe Vera applied topically can heal burns and wounds; stimulates cell regeneration; and has astringent, emollient, antifungal, antibacterial and antiviral properties. Taken internally, soothes stomach irritation, aids in healing, and has laxative properties. Good for AIDS and for skin and digestive disorders. Can be used either in juice or gel form.

Elder builds the blood cleanses the system, eases constipation, enhances immune systems function, fights inflammation, increases perspiration, lowers fever, soothes the respiratory tract, and stimulates circulation. Can be used in the form of tea or tincture/extract.

Peppermint enhances digestion by increasing stomach acidity; useful for chills, colic, diarrhea, headache, heart trouble, indigestion, nausea, poor appetite, rheumatism, and spasms. Can be used int eh form of tea.

Echinacea/Goldenseal is a good herbal formula and complement each other well. Echinacea has anti-inflammatory and antiviral properties. It is good for the immune system and the lymphatic system. Useful for colic, colds, flu, and other infectious illnesses. Also helpful for snakebite. Echinacea is also cut for skin wounds (cuts, insect bites, etc.) Goldenseal acts as an antibiotic, cleanses the body, increases the effectiveness of insulin, and strengthens the immune system; promotes the functioning capacity of the colon, liver, pancreas, spleen, and the lymphatic and respiratory systems. It cleanses mucous membranes, counter infection, improves digestion, and regulates menses; also decreases uterine bleeding, reduces blood pressure, and stimulates the central nervous system. Goldenseal is goodfor inflammation, ulcers, and any infectious dis-ease. Used the first sign of possible symptoms, it can stop a cold, flu, or sore throat from developing. Do not take Goldenseal for more than 7 consecutive days at a time. Can use in tincture/extract from. Can also use powder of Goldenseal topically for cuts, athlete's foot and other fungal infections.

Lavender relieves stress and depression, and is beneficial for the skin, good for burns, headaches, psoriasis, and skin problems. Can be used in tea form or add essential oil to baths or baths and beauty products.

Skullcap aids sleep, improves circulation, and strengthens the heart muscle; good for anxiety, fatigue, cardiovascular disease, headache, hyperactivity, nervous disorders, and rheumatism; relieves muscles cramps, pain, spasms, and stress; useful in treating barbiturate addiction and drug withdrawal. Can be used int eh form of a tincture/ext-act, capsules or in tea.

Nettle is a diuretic, expectorant, pain reliever, and tonic; contains vital minerals that are essential in
other allergic disorders, kidney problems,
atory conditions, and mucous conditions
xtract or capsules.

omach, intestines, liver and heart, useful
f d bleeding. It is used to stop either internal or external bleeding and to promote healing of burns and torn flesh. Can be used in the form of a tincture/extract or capsules. Can be used topically as a douche for vaginal discharge and hemorrhoids.

And God said, "Behold, I have given you every herb bearing see, which is upon the face of all the earth, and every tree, in which the fruit of a yielding seed, to you it shall be for meat." Genesis 1

Ten Common Homeopathic Medicines

By Dana Ullman MPH

If you wish to experiment with homeopathic medicines, here are ten medicines that are used for common ailments...and you can purchase any of these medicines from us HERE or simply email what you want to us at:email@homeopathic.com

These medicines should be taken in the 6th or 30th potency. Generally, if there is minor pain or discomfort, you should take the medicine three times a day, stopping once health has been restored. If there is more severe the pain, you can consider taking the medicine every one to three hours, decreasing the doses as symptoms are reduced. If you do not observe some improvement after 24 hours in an acute condition, the medicine is probably not the correct one. If symptoms persist, consider another medicine, or seek professional homeopathic care.

It is generally recommended that people treat themselves for non-threatening acute conditions only and obtain professional care for chronic or potential dangerous health conditions. Dr. Stephen Cummings and Dana Ullman's

Everybody's Guide to Homeopathic Medicines (Tarcher/Putnam, 2004) provides detailed protocols for helping to determine when symptoms are beyond self-care.

Allium cepa (onion): Because it is known to cause tearing of the eyes and dripping of the nose, it is a frequent remedy for the common cold and hay fever, especially when there is a thin, watery, and burning nasal discharge that irritates the nostrils. Typically, the person's symptoms are worse in a warm room and are relieved in a cool room or in the open air.

Arnica (mountain daisy): This is the #1 remedy in sports medicine and first aid. It is used for shock and trauma from injury. It also helps to reduce pain from injury and to speed the healing process. Whether you're into competitive sports or exercise regularly or if you simply don't like to feel the pain of an injury, Arnica is the place to start.

Arnica (topical): The above use of Arnica is for internal consumption, usually in pill or pellet form. Another way to use Arnica is in a topical external application 30

in a gels, ointment, or spray form. This application of Arnica is great for healing sprains and strains as well as black and blue bruising (without broken skin).

Chamomilla (chamomille): Many parents owe their sleep to homeopathy, not because it helps them directly, but because it is so good for their infant. **Chamomilla** is THE remedy for the irritable infant, especially from teething or colic. The infant cries incessantly, and nothing seems to provide any relief, except carrying them, and even then, the crying begins recurs as soon as the parent puts the child down.

Hypericum (St. John's wort): This remedy is the first medicine to consider for injuries to the nerves or to parts of the body rich with them, including the fingers, toes, and back. Any injury with shooting pains should be given this remedy.

Ignatia (St. Ignatius bean): One day this remedy will be used by the majority of psychiatrists. It is one of the leading homeopathic medicines for acute grief, anxiety, and depression, especially after a death or separation from a loved one. The person sighs frequently, has a lump in the throat, and may tremble.

Magnesia phosphorica (phosphate of magnesia): This is the most effective remedy for cramps, including menstrual cramps. It has helped prevent many women turn from Dr. Jekkyl into Ms. Hyde as a result of menstrual cramps. It is particularly indicated when a woman's cramps cause her to bend over and when they experience some relief from warm applications.

Nux vomica (poison nut): This is the premier medicine for ailments exacerbated by conventional or recreational drugs. It is also a common remedy for treating symptoms of overeating or from drinking too much alcohol. Considering how many people have these vices, this is an all too frequent medicine today.

Pulsatilla (windflower): Perhaps the most common remedy given to both children and women, this medicine is not indicated for a specific disease but for a specific pattern of physical symptoms and psychological characteristics. Physically, these people are warm-blooded: they wear less clothes than others, prefer open air, and don't feel as well in the heat. Psychologically, they are a gentle, mind, and yielding person, with a quickly changing emotional state and a strong tendency to want to please others.

Rhus tox (poison ivy): This medicine is the most common remedy for sprains and strains. It is especially indicated when a person experiences a "rusty gate" syndrome, that is, pain on initial motion which is reduced the more theperson continues to move. It is also often given to people with the flu or arthritis who experience this similar rusty gate syndrome.

Common Remedies for a Homeopathic First Aid Kit

- Aconite (Monkshood) psychic shock, unfounded fears, symptoms may occur after great fears, stress, chills, accidents, or sudden & dramatic changes in weather.
- Apis mellifica (Bee venom) tissues are edematous, red, hot and painful from insect bites, allergies.
- Bellladonna (Deadly Nightshade) sudden high fever, redness pain, thirstlessness, dilated pupils and panting, heatstroke, bright red, painful ears in children who wake up in pain, migraine headaches with extreme sensitivity to light & noise, red eruptions on the skin with high fevers.
- Calendula (Marigold Flower) wounds and cuts, infections-tinctures, washes, ointments, and creams to prevent and treat infections.
- Cantharis (Blister beetle) primarily for first- and second- degree blistered burns but also indicated in cystitis with burning and urging to urinate.

- Carbo vegetabilis (Vegetable carbon) bloating & conditions of trapped gas in the intestinal tract, colic, volvulus, gastric torsions and distensions; collapse near death with pale and/or blue mucous membranes. (Corpse Revival Remedy)
- Ledum (Marsh Tea) puncture wounds including bite wounds, cactus spines, injections, insect stings especially when affected part is cold & made better by cold applications.
- Millefolium (Yarrow) indicated in cases of profuse hemorrhage of bright red blood.
- Rhus Tox (Poison Ivy or Poison Oak) skin symptoms, osteoarthritis, strains and sprains in the joints, better with movement and worse for rest, flu symptoms.
- Ruta Grav (Rue)-strains, sprains and bruising of the ligaments and tendons which is worse with movement.
- Silicea (Silica) for resolving abscesses. The abscesses of Silicea are slow to suppurate. Silicea will either force the abscess to drain or be absorbed. Will eventually force the expulsion of foreign bodies, splinters, etc.
- Symphytum (Comfrey Root) Broken bones both acutely and in fractured delayed union fractures to speed healing, also indicated for bone pain post healing and blunt trauma to the eye during healing. (Do not use withbroken bones until in alignment and stabilized)

FLU REMEDIES

- Oscillococcinum (Duck Liver) Often first choice for flu and respiratory symptoms; available at drugstores, grocery stores, health food stores; Do not need to take entire vial asstated on the box, 7-8 pellets under the tongue will do; take at very first symptoms and continue every 4 to 6hours.
- Arsenicum Alba (Arsnic) Covers more phases of flu than any other remedy and will decrease symptoms especially with copious nasal flow and prostration. Suited for the early symptoms when the affection is in the upper portion of the respiratorytract.

  Burning dryness & copious watery excoriating secretion & involvement of the conjunctiva are also indications.

- Bryonia (White Bryony) Consider when symptoms are worse from motion of any kind; Tends toward dryness of the mucous membranes with great thirst for large quantities of cold fluids. Tends to be irritable and prefers to be left alone.
- Eupatorium Perfoliatum (Boneset) Deep aching, often felt in the bones. May feel as if their bones are broken. Eyes can also be quite sore. Frequently have a chill between 7:00 AM & 9:00 AM
- Gelsemium (Yellow Jessamine) Indicated at the beginning of symptoms, weak, tired & aches throughout the body, headache back of head, stiffness in neck, symptoms worse with movement, constant chilliness, heat & cold may alternate. One of the most commonly used flu remedies41

Healthy Diets - Food as Medicine

Food for Healing

'The wise man should consider that health is the greatest of human blessings.

Let food be your medicine.'—Hippocrates

Changing our eating habits can prove difficult. Sudden changes will surely lead to failure. Small steps are usually the best approach. Begin by evaluating your current needs, health challenges and lifestyle. Consider incorporating the small changes listed below:

- drink water instead of sodas and juices, alkaline or distilled water are good options
- reduce or limit meat and dairy consumption by replacing animal protein with plant-based proteins
- reduce or eliminate sugary and high-glycemic foods (avoid hidden sugars in foods and follow the Glycemic Index)
- sweeten drinks, desserts, and other foods with natural sweeteners like agave nectar, monk fruit, xylitol, stevia. Sweeteners such as honey, maple syrup are high glycemic foods and elevate blood sugar.
- replace ordinary table salt with Celtic or Himalayan salt, kelp or herbs and spices.

- practice good food combing for proper digestion (combing proteins with vegetables and starches with vegetables; combining proteins and starches together is a poor food combination and interferes with properdigestion
- include liquid meals such as freshly juiced vegetables and/or smoothiesdaily
- eat fresh, unprocessed foods, avoiding foods with hydrogenated oils, monosodium glutamate (MSG) and high fructose corn syrup or other artificial sweeteners
- include nutrient-dense foods (superfoods) in your diet daily
- include herbs and foods that contain vitamins and minerals into the diet to avoid dependency on synthetic vitamin and mineral supplements
- eat your last meal 2 hours prior to bedtime to avoid interference w th the digestive process
- replace black and white teas with herbal teas such as alfalfa, peppermint, pau d'arco, catnip, oat straw, red raspberry, nettle andhorsetail
- eat organic foods whenever possible (when organic is not possible at least avoid the "Dirty Dozen" --produce that are grown with heavy amounts of pesticides such as celery, strawberries, spinach, cherries, grapes, apples, peaches, pears, nectarines, tomatoes, bell and hot peppers, kale/mustard/collard greens)
- cook in iron, stainless steel, glass, or porcelain cookware, avoiding aluminum pans and utensils

Healthy Diet Choices

Below are some healthy diets to consider, though not every diet is for everybody. Before changing your diet, always consult your healthcare provider, especially if diagnosed with a serious illness or you are pregnant.

* **Raw Food Diet**

The raw food diet, also known as raw foodism or raw veganism, is comprised of mostly or completely raw and unprocessed foods (fruits, vegetables, nuts and seeds). A food is considered to be raw if it is never heated over 104-118 degrees Fahrenheit. These foods should also be unrefined, unpasteurized, and not treated with pesticides or processed in any other way. Food is usually prepared by dehydrating, blending, juicing, soaking, and sprouting. This diet usually increases one's energy levels and your general well-being quickly. Some report relief from migraines and other pain, less bloating and weight loss.

* **Juicing or Juice Fasting**

Juicing is the process of consuming raw fruits and vegetables by using a juicer that either squeezes, pulverizes or crushes. Freshly pressed juice made from raw (unprocessed) fruits and vegetables, provides the easiest and most effective way of providing high quality nutrition to the body. This promotes a healthy immune system which is then able to ward off disease and discomfort. By juicing, one can take in the nutrients and enzymes from nearly 15 pounds of produce every day, in a form that is easy to digest and absorb. Juicing may be done by a Juice Feast (adding glass of fresh juice to your usual meal) in order to increase your nutritional intake of vitamins, minerals and antioxidants. Juicing may also be incorporated into the diet by a Juice Fast (using a 3–10- day juice cleanse with only fresh juices as your meals). This can help to flush your body of harmful toxins while allowing your digestive system a break. This should be done under consultation of your health care provider as it may be contraindicated for somepeople.

* **Alkaline Diet**

The Alkaline Diet (aka the Acid-Alkaline or Alkaline-Ash Diet) is based the theory that acid- forming foods make the body more vulnerable to illness and disease, where the alkaline- forming foods are more healing and protective. The body's pH reflects how healthy we are - balancing the body pH, is a major step toward well- being and greater health. Thus, choosing more alkaline foods or "alkalizing" the body improves your health. Supporters of this diet proport that at least 70% of the diet should include alkaline-forming foods, which are fruits, nuts, legumes, and vegetables (acid-forming foods include meat,poultry, fish, dairy, eggs, grains, and alcohol).

* **The Macrobiotic Diet**

The Macrobiotic Diet is a strict diet which follows the Yin- Yang concept of healing. The diet is primarily consisting of organic whole grains (brown rice, barley, oats, buckwheat) up to half of your food intake, locally grown,

organic fruits and vegetables for up to a quarter of your food intake, and soups made with vegetables, seaweed beans, chickpeas, lentils, fermented soyfor up to a quarter of your food intake. The mac robiotic way isto approach sickness by restoring a condition of harmony and balance. It is more than a diet, it is a way of life (having restrictions on when you eat and drink, how your food is prepared, stored, and reheated and more)

SUPER FOODS

Superfoods are generally considered to be foods that contact high levels of much- needed vitamins and minerals. These nutrient-dense foods can also be a source of antioxidants, substances that shield the body from cell damage and help prevent disease. Some of these foods may be common, easily accessible items while others may be more exotic and less mainstream. A list of both is providedhere:

- Almonds
- Broccoli Rabe
- Avocados
- Wheatgrass
- Salmon
- Flaxseeds
- Blueberries
- Cinnamon
- Sweet Potatoes
- Acai Berries
- Goji Berries
- Cacao/Cocoa Powder
- Seaweed
- Chia Seeds
- Mangosteens
- Maca Powder

THE BENEFITS OF COLLOIDAL SILVER

1. ANTIVIRAL
2. ANTIBACTERIAL
3. HELPS WITH WOUND HEALING
4. BENEFITS SKIN CONDITIONS
5. TREATS EAR INFECTIONS
6. TREATS PINK EYE
7. ANTI-INFLAMMATORY
8. FIGHTS SINUS INFECTIONS
9. ELIMINATES AND PREVENTS COMMON COLDS
10. ELIMINATES AND PREVENTS ALL TYPES OF FLU
11. FIGHTS BRONCHITIS
12. FIGHTS PNEUMONIA

WELLNESSPROFILE.ORG

9 FOOD-SUPPLEMENTS THAT BOOST YOUR CALCIUM

by Yuma "Docta Yew" Bellomee

Calcium is an essential mineral that is typically best obtained from food. Calcium works as a strengthener for nerves, muscle movement, metabolism, bones, and teeth. It is needed for the heart to pump blood, for hormonal release & function, for moderating acid levels in the body, and for preventing bone loss & easy fractures. Here are some great foods that can potentially be implemented to help bring our calcium levels up.

1. **Sea Moss** - Blend the gel or the powder into beverages, hot cereals, or desserts. The calcium found in sea moss is more easily absorbed than many calcium supplements, and sea moss also contains other nutrients that may aid calcium absorption.

2. **Raw Carob Powder** - Add to smoothies, cereals, or desserts. Carob powder has a naturally sweet flavor, so besides it being a good food source of calcium, it can also help to reduce the amount of sugar you'd want to use in some of your recipes. Concentrated, refined sugars are known to deplete the body of calcium.

3. **Chia Seeds** - Add to beverages, salad dressings, or cereals. Chia seeds are often used as a thickener in recipes, egg replacer for holding baked goods together, and as a nutritional aid. Besides containing calcium, it also contains bone supportive nutrients such as Omega-3 and boron. Other edible seeds that provide abundant calcium include black sesame seeds and sachainchi seeds.

4. **Amaranth** - Instead of the popular corn grits or oatmeal, the cooked amaranth seeds can be substituted in meals. It is richer in calcium than most other cereal grains and is also a source of complete protein.

5. **Navy Beans** - Eat as a protein with vegetables. Navy beans and other white beans are rich in calcium, magnesium, and fiber, which aid healthy metabolism and elimination.

6. **Moringa Leaf Powder** - Add to salad dressings, water, broths, or vegetable juices. Moringa has a multitude of beneficial nutrients, including approximately 60 mg of calcium in a generous teaspoonful of thepowder.

7. **Blackstrap Molasses** - Add to water or use to sweeten foods and beverages. Blackstrap molasses is the storehouse of nutrients that sugar

cane naturally contains before it's stripped during sugar refinement. Just one tablespoon of blackstrap molasses offers about 100 mg ofcalcium.

8. **Greens** - Eat raw or steamed. Turnip greens, collard greens, dandelion greens, and other dark green leafy vegetables are also rich in calcium, iron, and Vitamins A & K - all needed for strong bones and blood vessels.

9. **Sunlight** - Most of us don't think of sunlight as a food, but the primary way our bodies produce Vitamin D is through direct sunlight exposure on our skins. Vitamin D is necessary for the proper absorption and utilization of calcium in our bodies. At least 30 minutes of sunlight exposure daily is also linked to improved immune response, mood, and hormonal balance.

Yuma "Docta Yew" Bellomee is a Certified Holistic Health Consultant, Herbalist, Wholistic Wellness Advocate, Healing Workshop Facilitator and Performing Artist

Acupuncture

Acupuncture involves the insertion of very thin needles through your skin at strategic points on your body. A key component of traditional Chinese medicine, acupuncture is most commonly used to treat pain.

Increasingly, it is being used for overall wellness, including stress management.

Traditional Chinese medicine explains acupuncture as a technique for balancing the flow of energy or life force — known as chi or qi (chee) — believed to flow through pathways (meridians) in your body. By inserting needles into specific points along these meridians, acupuncture practitioners believe that your energy flow will re-balance.

In contrast, many Western practitioners view the acupuncture points as places to stimulate nerves, muscles and connective tissue. Some believe that this stimulation boosts your body's natural painkillers.

Acupuncture is used mainly to relieve discomfort associated with a variety of diseases and conditions, including:

- Chemotherapy-induced and postoperative nausea and vomiting
- Dental pain
- Headaches, including tension headaches and migraines
- Labor pain
- Low back pain
- Neck pain
- Osteoarthritis
- Menstrual cramps
- Respiratory disorders, such as allergic rhinitis

Source: MayoClinic.org

Unique Scripts--Reflexology, Vibrational Sound Therapy, Functional Medicine and Yoni Steam by

Sheila L. Hall

Reflexology is an alternative medicine involving application of pressure to the feet and hands with specific thumb, finger, and hand techniques without the use of oil or lotion. It is based on a system of zones and reflex areas that purportedly reflect an image of the body on the feet and hands, with the premise that such work effects a physical change to the body.

Vibrational Sound Therapy (VST) combines powerful vibration and tones to induce an immediate relaxed state. The induction of the sound waves directly into the body, along with soothing ambient tones, is such a strong treatment that clients report effects ranging from a meditative state to deep relaxation. By placing the "therapeutic" singing bowls directly on the body, and using correct techniques, a practitioner engages with their client both physically, and aurally. Also known as vibrational sound massage

This Treatment in highly recommended for those you are experiencing trouble sleeping, high stress and circulatory imbalances.

Functional Medicine is a systems biology–based approach that focuses on identifying and addressing the root cause of disease. Each symptom or differential diagnosis may be one of many contributing to an individual'sillness.

Yoni Steam is a bath that sends an aromatic blend of warm herbal steam gently through the vagina and cervix, into the fallopian tubes, ovaries and uterus. The herbs, flowers and spices used are carefully selected to help fortify, cleanse, detox, strengthen, and tone a women's most intimate and loving parts. Some of the reported benefits of yoni steaming include:

- reducing menstrual symptoms, such as bloating,
- cramps, exhaustion, and heavy bleeding
- boosting fertility
- promoting healing after childbirth
- reducing stress
- treating hemorrhoids
- increasing energy and reducing fatigue
- treating headaches

Sheila Lavonne, also known as "The MAD Coach" is the owner of Unique Scripts Wellness Spa and Juice Bar. Sheila helps women entrepreneurs who are experiencing debilitating menopausal symptoms, which she calls "Menopausal Affective Disorder" aka – M.A.D., to get relief holistically in order to bring balance into their life, physically, mentally and within their business. I also specialize in trauma induced hormonal imbalances, stress and pain management. My motto is: "Wellness is not exclusive, it's inclusive, to your business, so don't get mad about it!" The MAD Coach also help women eliminate their Fibroids, endometriosis, pelvic pain and Infertility through a transformative holistic approach of spirit, mind, body healing--leveraging coaching, nutrition change, herbal supplements, holistic practices and medical Qi Gong. From stress management to diet and more, the program teaches lifestyle changes and feeling good to live your bestlife.

Chiropractic Medicine

Chiropractic is . . .

a health-care profession that focuses on the spine and other joints of the body, and their connection to the nervous system. The word "chiropractic" means "to be done by hand." Chiropractors use adjustments to restore joint function and support the nervous system. They help patients maintain optimal health while avoiding unnecessary drugs or surgery. An estimated 50 million Americans see a chiropractor each year.

A chiropractor is . . .

a primary care doctor who specializes in spinal health and well-

being. They focus on the prevention, diagnosis and conservative care of spine- related disorders and other painful joint issues. In addition to adjustments, chiropractors also provide soft-tissue therapies,

lifestyle recommendations, fitness coaching and nutritional advice. A

chiropractic adjustment is . . .

a very safe, specific, controlled force applied to a joint to restore proper function and mobility. Accidents, falls, stress or overexertion can negatively impact your spine or other joints. These changes impact tissues, the nervous system and other areas of the body. Left unresolved, this can make you more susceptible to chronic

problems. Chiropractic adjustments reduce pain, increase movement and improve performance.

Chiropractors collaborate . . .

with other health-care providers every day. They are trained to refer you to the appropriate specialist when needed.

Chiropractors use . . .

scientific research, clinical experience, and patient preferences to provide the best care possible. Ninety-five percent of past-year chiropractic users say it's effective, and 89 percent recommend chiropractic to their family andfriends.

Chiropractic is safe, effective, affordable care.

Why Choose It?

Chiropractic is the method of natural healing most chosen by those seeking complementary/alternative health care for acute and chronic conditions.

While you may first visit a chiropractor to relieve pain in the lower back

or to treat sciatica, neck pain, whiplash or headache, you will find that a chiropractor views you as a whole person and not the sum of your parts. A chiropractor will work in partnership with you to ensure your optimal health and wellness.

TRIGGERS YOUR BODY'S ABILITY TO HEAL

Chiropractors recognize that many factors affect your health, including exercise, nutrition, sleep, environment and heredity. Chiropractic focuses on maintaining your health naturally to help your body resist disease, rather than simply treating the symptoms of disease.

STARTS WITH A THOROUGH EVALUATION

When you visit a Doctor of Chiropractic, you will be evaluated using time-honored methods, including consultation, case history, physical examination, laboratory analysis and X-ray examination. In addition, you will receive a careful chiropractic structural examination, with particular attention paid to the spine.

INVOLVES NO DRUGS OR SURGERY

A broad range of techniques are used to locate, analyze and gently correct vertebral misalignments (subluxations) in the spine.

Chiropractors may use manual adjustment, electrical muscular stimulation, ultrasound or massage. But they never use pharmaceutical drugs or invasive surgery. Chiropractic is a natural method of healing that stimulates the body's communication system to work more effectively to initiate, control and coordinate the various functions of the cells, organs and systems of the body.

PARTNERS WITH OTHER HEALTHCARE PROFESSIONALS

Doctors of chiropractic work in tandem with other healthcare professionals. If your condition requires attention from another branch of the healthcare profession, that recommendation or referral will be made. (Source: Palmer College of Chiropractic)

Signs of a Heart Attack: Catch the signs early

Don't wait to get help if you experience any of these heart attack warning signs. Some heart attacks are sudden and intense. But most start slowly, with mild pain or discomfort. Pay attention to your body and call 911 if you experience:

- Chest discomfort. Most heart attacks involve discomfort in the center of the chest that lasts more than a few minutes – or it may go away and then return. It can feel like uncomfortable pressure, squeezing, fullness orpain.
- Discomfort in other areas of the upper body. Symptoms can include pain or discomfort in one or both arms, the back, neck, jaw orstomach.
- Shortness of breath. This can occur with or without chest discomfort.
- Other signs. Other possible signs include breaking out in acold
- sweat, nausea or lightheadedness.

Source: American Heart Association

Signs of a Stroke

F.A.S.T. Warning Signs

Use the letters in F.A.S.T to spot a Stroke

- **F = Face Drooping** – Does one side of the face droop or is it numb?Ask the person to smile. Is the person's smile uneven?
- **A = Arm Weakness** – Is one arm weak or numb? Ask the person to raise both arms. Does one arm drift downward?
- **S = Speech Difficulty** – Is speech slurred?
- **T = Time to call 911**

Other Stroke Symptoms Watch

for Sudden:

- NUMBNESS or weakness of face, arm, or leg, especially on one side of thebody
- CONFUSION, trouble speaking or understanding speech
- TROUBLE SEEING in one or both eyes
- TROUBLE WALKING, dizziness, loss of balance or coordination
- SEVERE HEADACHE with no known cause

Source: American Stroke Association

Diabetes Symptoms

Get your blood sugar tested if you have any of the symptoms of diabetes. If you have any of the following diabetes symptoms, see your doctor about getting your blood sugar tested:

- Urinate (pee) a lot, often at night
- Are very thirsty
- Lose weight without trying
- Are very hungry
- Have blurry vision
- Have numb or tingling hands or feet
- Feel very tired
- Have very dry skin
- Have sores that heal slowly
- Have more infections than usual

Source: Centers for Disease Control and Prevention

HERBS THAT LOWER BLOOD SUGAR
Cinnamon
Cloves
Rosemary
Oregano
Sage
Curry Leaves
Garlic
Ginger
Turmeric
Cayenne
Marjoram

Symptoms of Severe High Blood Pressure

If your blood pressure is extremely high, there may be certain symptoms to look out for, including:

- Severe headaches
- Nosebleed
- Fatigue or confusion
- Vision problems
- Chest pain
- Difficulty breathing
- Irregular heartbeat
- Blood in the urine
- Pounding in your chest, neck, or ears

People sometimes feel that other symptoms may be related to high blood pressure, but they may not be:

- Dizziness
- Nervousness
- Sweating
- Trouble sleeping
- Facial flushing
- Blood spots in eyes

Source: WebMD.com

Physical symptoms of stress include:

- Aches and pains.
- Chest pain or a feeling like your heart is racing.
- Exhaustion or trouble sleeping.
- Headaches, dizziness or shaking.
- High blood pressure.
- Muscle tension or jaw clenching.
- Stomach or digestive problems.
- Trouble having sex.
- Weak immune system.

Stress can lead to emotional and mental symptoms like:

- Anxiety or irritability.
- Depression.
- Panic attacks.
- Sadness.

What are some strategies for stress relief?

You can't avoid stress, but you can stop it from becoming overwhelming by practicing some daily strategies:

- Exercise when you feel symptoms of stress comingon. Even a short walk can boost your mood.
- At the end of each day, take a moment to think about what you've accomplished — not what you didn't get done.
- Set goals for your day, week and month. Narrowing your view will helpyou feel more in control of the moment and long-termtasks.
- Consider talking to a therapist or your healthcare provider aboutyour worries.

What are some ways to prevent stress?

Many daily strategies can help you keep stress at bay:

- Try relaxation activities, such as meditation, yoga, tai chi, breathing exercises and muscle relaxation. Programs are available online, in smartphone apps, and at many gyms and communitycenters.
- Take good care of your body each day. Eating right, exercising andgetting enough sleep help your body handle stress muchbetter.
- Stay positive and practice gratitude, acknowledging the good parts ofyour day or life.
- Accept that you can't control everything. Find ways to let go ofworryabout situations you cannot change.
- Learn to say "no" to additional responsibilities when you are too busyor stressed.
- Stay connected with people who keep you calm, make you happy,provide emotional support and help you with practical things. A friend, family member or neighbor can become a good listener or share responsibilities so that stress doesn't become overwhelming.

Source: ClevelandClinic.org

Reflect.
A Soulful Touch

Signs of Toxicity (Poisoning)

General symptoms

General symptoms of poisoning can include:

- feeling and being sick
- diarrhea
- stomach pain
- drowsiness, dizziness or weakness
- high temperature
- chills (shivering)
- loss of appetite
- headache
- irritability
- difficulty swallowing (dysphagia)
- breathing difficulties
- producing more saliva than normal
- skin rash
- blue lips and skin (cyanosis)
- burns around the nose or mouth
- double vision or blurred vision
- mental confusion
- seizures (fits)
- loss of consciousness
- coma, in severe cases

Source: NHS.UK

Black Survival: Growing Food and Healing Herbs

With the global pandemic, various parts of the planet have experienced food shortages. As a means of survival, we encourage our people to grow foods (fruits, vegetables, grains, and herbs) when and where possible. This guide has provided a list of herbs and superfoods that provide optimal nutrition and healing herbs. Feel free to begin with one or a few of these foods to secure and maintain your family/community's food supply. The USA and Africa zone maps can serve as a guide to determine your growing zone for prime times to grow plants based on your climate's region.

Vegetable suggestions for warm and cool climates/seasons

Warm-weather vegetables usually thrive in summer month with a lot of sunlight. These include:

- Cucumbers
- Tomatoes
- Peppers
- Squash
- Sorrels
- Beans
- Greens
- Berries
- Sweet Potatoes
- Southern Peas
- Okra
- Manoa Lettuce
- Eggplant
- Amaranth
- Malabar Spinach
- Corn
- Melons
- Shallots

Cool-season veggies grow best at temperatures averaging lower than those needed by warm season types. Many have edible leaves or roots like:

- Lettuce
- Spinach
- Carrots
- Radishes
- Broccoli
- Cauliflower
- Peas

To recommend Black-owned and Black-Friendly Farms, go to www.iloveblackpeople.com

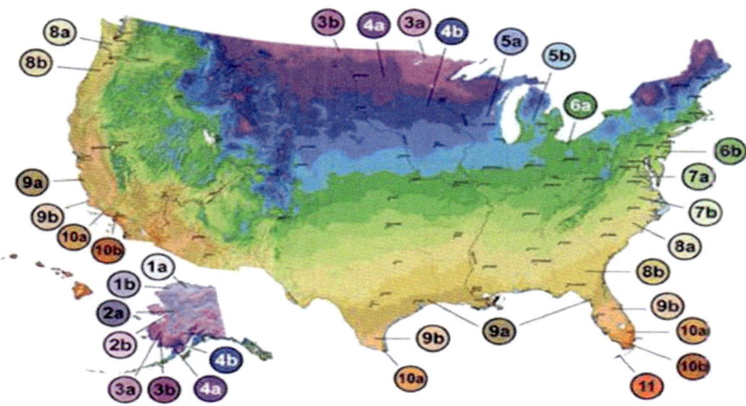

Before planting,

KNOW YOUR ZONE!

Posted by Brooks Wilson on 6/7/2017 to Landscaping Calculators & Charts

Every type of plant has a low temperature threshold. The USDA Plant Hardiness Zones help gardeners and landscapers understand which plants will most likely survive the average low winter temperatures at a specific location. They also indicate how far south in the United States a specific plant will likely grow.

USDA ZONE MAP

To use the map, find your location to see what color it is in and then find the number that corresponds to the color of that zone.

Zone Descriptions

Zone 1 | below -50 F

Zone 1 has a low temperature of below -50 Fahrenheit and below -45.6 Celsius, covering interior areas of Alaska, Resolute, Northwest Territories of Canada, northernmost tip of China.

Zone 2a | -50 to -45 F
Zone 2a has a low temperature of -50 to -45 Fahrenheit and -42.8 to -45.5 Celsius, spanning from interior areas of Alaska, northern regions of Canada (Manitoba), and northernmost isolated parts of China.

Zone 2b | -45 to -40 F
Zone 2b has a low temperature of -45 to -40 Fahrenheit and -40 to -42.7 Celsius, spanning from interior areas of Alaska (Unalakleet), the northernmost tip of Minnesota, middle regions of Canada, and northernmost regions of China.

Zone 3a | -40 to -35 F
Zone 3a has a low temperature of -40 to -35 Fahrenheit and -37.3 to -39.9 Celsius, spanning from northernmost regions of Minnesota (International Falls), interior and northern coastal areas of Alaska (St. Michael), southern regions of Canada, northern regions of Europe, northern regions of China, and central regions of northern Japan.

Zone 3b | -35 to -30 F
Zone 3b has a low temperature of -35 to -30 Fahrenheit and -34.5 to -37.2 Celsius, spanning from northernmost regions of the US, interior and northern coastal areas of Alaska, southern regions of Canada, northern areas of Europe, some central and northern interior regions of China, and interior regions of northern Japan.

Zone 4a | -30 to -25 F
Zone 4a has a low temperature of -30 to -25 Fahrenheit and -31.7 to -34.4 Celsius, spanning from northern regions in the Midwest and northeast US, western coastal areas of Alaska, coastal regions of eastern Canada, northern areas of Europe, some central and northern interior regions of China, isolated areas of South America, and northern regions of Japan.

Zone 4b | -25 to -20 F
Zone 4b has a low temperature of -25 to -20 Fahrenheit and -28.9 to -31.6 Celsius, spanning from centrally located regions in the Midwest and northeast US, southern coastal areas of Alaska, coastal regions of eastern Canada, northern regions of Europe, some central and northern interior regions of China, southern regions of interior South America, and coastal regions of northern and interior regions of southern Japan.

Zone 5a | -20 to -15 F
Zone 5a has a low temperature of -20 to -15 Fahrenheit and -26.2 to -28.8 Celsius, spanning from central regions in the Midwest and lower regions of the northeast US, southern coastal areas of Alaska, coastal regions of western Canada, central interior regions of Europe, central and northern interior regions of China, southern interior regions of South America, and coastal regions of northern and interior regions of southern Japan.

Zone 5b | -15 to -10 F

Zone 5b has a low temperature of -15 to -10 Fahrenheit and -23.4 to -26.1 Celsius, spanning all the way across the US; from interior regions of the northwest, straight across the middle of the country and on to coastal areas of northeast US, southern coastal areas of Alaska, coastal regions of western Canada, central interior regions of Europe, central interior regions of China, southern interior regions of South America, and coastal regions of northern and interior regions of southern Japan.

Zone 6a | -10 to -5 F

Zone 6a has a low temperature of -10 to -5 Fahrenheit and -20.6 to -23.3 Celsius, spanning all the way across the US; from interior regions of the northwest to straight through the mid-US (St. Louis, Missouri) to southern Pennsylvania, southern coastal areas of Alaska, coastal regions of western Canada, central interior regions of Europe, central interior regions of China, southern regions of South America, and coastal regions of northern and interior regions of southern Japan.

Zone 6b | -5 to 0 F

Zone 6b has a low temperature of -5 to 0 Fahrenheit and -17.8 to -20.5 Celsius, spanning all the way across the US; from interior regions of the northwest across to northernmost areas of Tennessee on to the mid Atlantic coast, coastal regions of western Canada, central interior regions of Europe, central interior regions of China, southern regions of South America, and coastal regions of northern and central interior regions of southern Japan.

Zone 7a | 0 to 5 F

Zone 7a has a low temperature of 0 to 5 Fahrenheit and -15 to -17.7 Celsius, spanning all the way across the US; from northeast California across southern Oklahoma to up through the Appalachian Mountains to the mid Atlantic coast, coastal regions of western Canada, central interior regions of China, central interior regions of Europe, coastal regions of northern and central interior regions of southern Japan, and northern and southern interior regions of Africa.

Zone 7b | 5 to 10 F

Zone 7b has a low temperature of 5 to 10 Fahrenheit and -12.3 to -14.9 Celsius, spanning all the way across the US; from eastern California through southern New Mexico and central Texas, across the northern parts of Georgia and the Carolinas to the mid Atlantic coast, coastal regions of western Canada, central interior regions of Europe, central interior regions of China, coastal regions of northern and areas just inland in southern Japan southern interior regions of South America, and northern and southern interior regions of Africa.

Zone 8a | 10 to 15 F

Zone 8a has a low temperature of 10 to 15 Fahrenheit and -9.5 to -12 Celsius,spanning all the way across the US; from coastal areas of the northwest and California through central Arizona and Texas, across the southern halves and coasts of Mississippi, Alabama, Georgia and the Carolinas, central interior regions of Europe, central interior regions of China, coastal regions of southern Japan, southern interior regions of South America, and northern and southern interior regions of Africa.

Zone 8b | 15 to 20 F
Zone 8b has a low temperature of 15 to 20 Fahrenheit and -6.7 to -9.4 Celsius, spanning all the way across the US; from coastal areas of the northwest and California through central Arizona and southern Texas, to across south Georgia and north Florida, the southern interior region of southeast Australia, southern interior regions of Europe, central interior regions of China, coastal and areas just inland in southern Japan, and northern and southern interior regions of Africa.

Zone 9a | 20 to 25 F
Zone 9a has a low temperature of 20 to 25 Fahrenheit and -3.9 to -6.6 Celsius, covers areas of inland California and the Desert Southwest, southern Texas, and central Florida, southern regions of China, southern regions of Australia, coastal areas of southern Japan, and central regions to both the north and south of Africa.

Zone 9b | 25 to 30 F
Zone 9b has a low temperature of 25 to 30 Fahrenheit and -1.2 to -3.8 Celsius, covers interior regions of California and the Desert Southwest, southernmost Texas, and central Florida, southern regions of China, southern regions of Europe, a band that crosses the middle of Australia, coastal areas of southern Japan, and regions of southern Mexico and South America.

Zone 10a | 30 to 35 F
Zone 10a has a low temperature of 30 to 35 Fahrenheit and 1.6 to -1.1 Celsius, and covers areas of southernmost California and south Florida, southern regions of China, northern and southern coastal regions of Australia, southernmost coastal regions of Europe, interior and coastal regions of South America, and central and northern coastal regions of Africa.

Zone 10b | 35 to 40 F
Zone 10b has a low temperature of 35 to 40 Fahrenheit and 4.4 to 1.7 Celsius, covers areas of south Florida (Miami), southern most coastal regions of Europe (Portugal, Spain, and Italy), southernmost regions of China, northern regions of Australia, central regions of South and Central America, and interior and coastal regions of Africa.

Zone 11 | above 40 F
Zone 11 has a low temperature of above 40 Fahrenheit and above 4.5 Celsius, covers Hawaii (Honolulu), Southern Mexico, the Florida Keys, the northern most region of Australia, southernmost regions of China, northern regions of South America, coastal regions of Central America, and central interior and coastal areas of Africa.

Source:: https://www.wilsonbrosgardens.com

Africa Plant Hardiness Zone Map

Africa plant hardiness zones for gardeners. This map is based on the USDA Hardiness Zone Map, and the map covers Africa which ranges from Zone 2a to Zone 10b.

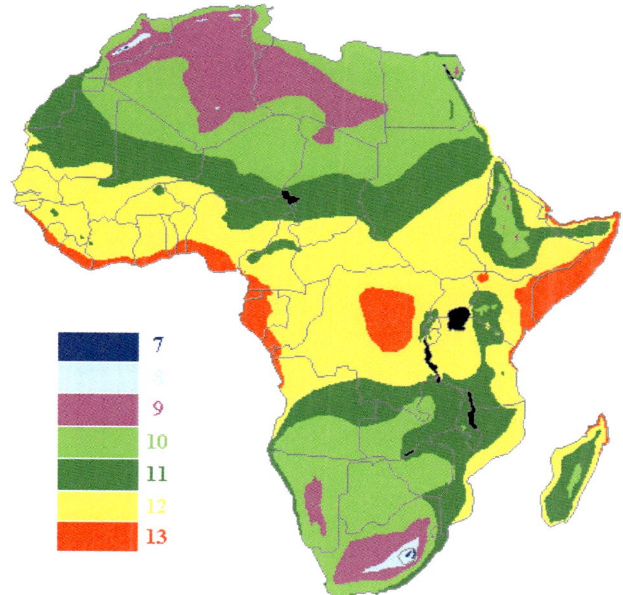

AFRICAN CLIMATE ZONES (based on av. coldest temp. in a winter)
Zone 7 = 0-9 deg F., 8=10-19 deg F., 9=20-29 deg F. [Created by Brandt Maxwell, 2001]
10=30-39 deg F., 11=40-49 deg F., 12=50-59 deg F., 13=60-69 deg F.

If you live outside North America

You can roughly translate the USDA hardiness zones by finding out how low your area's temperatures can reach, and then use the chart below to find your corresponding zone.

Source: https://www.backyardgardener.com/

Chapter 3: About Us

Greetings, and thank you for joining us on this journey.

We are building a global network to help protect Black people from racism & xenophobia, especially when they are most vulnerable, while traveling or in new environments. An even greater vulnerability when facing a global pandemic.

This is The Global Green Book 2020 Healthcare Edition: A Black Survival Guide. The goal of this book is to share the mission and spotlight Black liberation. Healthcare is highlighted in the midst of a pandemic and the challenges Black people face concerning health care decisions. We include a sampling of the safe healthcare providers listed on our online network.

These listings were gathered with the help of 500 I Love Black People ambassadors and over 50 000 members around the world. We have identified Black-Owned and Black Friendly health- care providers in more than 236 cities across theglobe.

However, we still need your help to identify more Black-owned & Black-friendly businesses inthe following categories: accommodation, food, transportation, legal, beauty, education/childcare, finance, and health. There are thousands of businesses that you may know and can recommend that we can add to ouronline network or the next publication of The Global Green Book. Your input will contribute to a global safety net protecting Black people from racism & xenophobia, especially when they are most vulnerable.

Like the original Green Book, we count on you to assist us with keeping it up to date and correct. These recommendations are crowdsourced, and we need the community to keep us current.

This guide will be revised and published annually. The Online Guide ILoveBlackPeople.com will be revised in real-time. If you find an error in our online listings, submit the correction in the review and we will make theupdate.

When visiting recommended businesses, mention ILoveBlackPeople.com to share how you found their place of business. If they have not heard about this guide, direct them to contact us and visit www.iloveblackpeople.com. Share with us how you stayed safe during COVID. Share how you recovered from COVID. Share the places you were welcomed and treated with dignity along the way. Healthcare professionals share with us the best practices for keeping our families and community safe. If this guide is useful, share it, If it's not useful, let us know. We encourage feedback, so we can continue to improve; and your feedback is greatly appreciated. Email: info@iloveblackpeople.com

We are identifying safe places around the globe to make sure that we protect our Black brothers and sisters from racism and xenophobia. The goal is to allow ourselves to share the good relationships that we have established in our communities. No matter where we are and where we live, we should be safe. The global pandemic has also changed our perception of safety. Knowing how to travel through life while Black is a life-or-death matter. These same sentiments prompted Victor Hugo Green, in 1936, during the height of Jim Crow segregation to write the "The Negro Motorists Green Book." A pocket- sized guide for African American travelers navigating racially segregated cities and the expandinghighwaysystem.

The original Green Book was a lifesaver for the courageous weary souls who fearlessly followed the sovereign call to strike out and explore their world. The Global Green Book accepts this challenge, understanding that "world" includes where we are now and where we may go in the future....and we continue this tradition.

Definitions

Colonialism

Today, African women and men are faced with inherent problems emanating from a crippling colonial system. Problems systematically produced by colonialism (in all forms). They have had ill-effects on people of African descent throughout the Globe. So, what exactly is colonialism in the context of people of Africandescent

To put it into proper perspective, a couple of explanations and definitions are provided below.

Classical Colonialism

Classical colonialism in Africa started centuries ago. Like the colonization of the Americas and the Atlantic Slave Trade, it was ushered in with systemic violence— organized, continuous, methodic, and willful. It was not only integral to capitalism, but also coexistent with racism, cultural domination *(Bulhan, 2008). Some ofthe lasting negative consequences of classical colonialism can be felt and observed within communities of African descent till this very day.

Neo-colonialism

The indirect control of a developing country's economic and political structure from outside of that country by a more developed country. Wherever colonialism has occurred and persists, it has created a void of an underdeveloped potential of its people, their cultures, and its communities. In turn, we have been left to engineer ways to circumvent the adverse effects of colonialism.

Knowing the problem of colonialism and its ill-effects presents us with an opportunity to address these problems head-on by introducing a new way of community and infrastructure building through actual rewarding acts of kindness.

Recognizing that many of the developmental issues faced by modern- day countries and communities of people of African descent stem from the concept of lack of "money" as a resource are no longer an excuse. We can no longer depend on money alone for the development of the people of African descent, but by leveraging our social and human capital. I Love Black People is a crowdsourced platform; we relyon people like you to build our network that supports Black people.

"The development of a country is brought about by people, not by money. Money andthe wealth it represents is the result and not the basis of development."

- J. Nyerere, 1967 The Arusha Declaration

White Supremist Ideology

Belief that White people are racially superior to others and should therefore dominate society.

Racism

Racism is the belief that a particular race is superior or inferior to another, that a person's social and moral traits are predetermined by his or her inborn biological characteristics. Race is not real and has its basis in pseudoscience not biology.

---

1 * Bulhan, Hussein A . 2015. Stages of C olonialism in A frica: F rom O ccupation of Land to O ccupation if Being. J Social & Political P sy chology .3(1): 239-256

Xenophobia

The fear or hatred of foreigners or strangers; it is embodied in discriminatory attitudes and behavior, and often culminates in violence, abuses of all types, and exhibitions of hatred. Such hatred is usually caused by the fear of loss of social status, and identity; a threat, perceived or real, to citizens' economic success, a way of reassuring the national self and its boundaries in times of national crisis.

Afrophobia

A range of negative attitudes and feelings towards Black people or people of African Descent around the world. Definitions refer to irrational fear, with the implication of antipathy, contempt and aversion. The term "afrophobia" is observable in discrimination and racist violence on the basis of a person's skin color, ethnic origin, and nationality.

Jim Crow Segregation

A practice or policy of segregating or discriminating against Black people, as in public places, public vehicles, or employment.

Genocide

The term refers to the deliberate intentional killing of a large number of people from a particular nation or ethnic group with the aim of destroying that nation orgroup.

Self-determination

The process by which a group of people form their own state and choose their own government;in other words, this is when a country determines its own statehood and forms its own government. Self- determination means complete sovereignty of a nation.

Ubuntu

Ubuntu can be described as the capacity in African culture to express compassion, reciprocity, dignity, humanity, and mutuality in the interests of building, and maintaining communities with justice, and is often translated as "I am because WE are," or "humanity towards others". Also commonly used in a more philosophical sense to mean "the belief in a universal bond of sharing that connects all humanity," i.e., mutual caring.

Chapter 4:

Background of the Green Book

The Grand African is not only known as the original human but also the original traveler. We navigated the many rivers, trails, and oceans of the world and impacted human existence on every continent. Unfortunately, our travels havenot always been positive experiences or welcomed. In many places across the globe, people of African descent, especially those of the darker hue, battle institutional and interpersonal discrimination. Knowing how to travel while Black has become a life-saving practice.

In 1936, during the height of Jim Crow segregation in the United States of America, Victor Hugo Green wrote his first edition of the “The Negro Motorists Green Book.” The pocket-sized Green book was a reference book for African-American travelers to use while navigating racially segregated cities and expandinghighways.

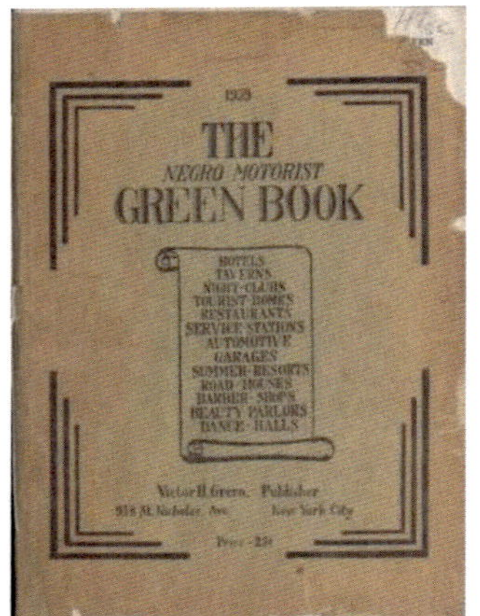

The Green Book was a directory of businesses that were welcoming to Black consumers; it also offered life- saving tips for avoiding discrimination and hate crimes. The Green Book helped Black travelers navigate through America with pride while also creating opportunities for the economic advancement of businesses that were Black-owned or supported Civil Rights. Unfortunately, the end to legalized discrimination did not ended facto discrimination, nor did it ensure the protection of humanrights.

THE
NEGRO MOTORIST

VICTOR H. GREEN
GEORGE L. SMITH

GREEN BOOK

1937 EDITION

INTRODUCTION

The idea of "The Green Book" is to compile facts and information connected with motoring, which the Negro Motorist can use and depend upon.

We are appealing to the Motorist and Business places for their whole-hearted co-operation to help us in our endeavor, by contributing ideas, suggestions, Travel information and articles of interest.

Every medium and resource is being used to contact Reliable Business Places and Resorts that will serve your motoring needs. All advertisements contained in this book has been carefully selected and we feel sure that your patronage will be appreciated by the advertisers.

In the event that you are dissatisfied with the service rendered by an advertiser, we would appreciate you writing us the complaint, stating all the facts and conditions and we will immediately investigate your case and help to adjust same.

Let's all get together and make Motoring better.

Published yearly in the month of May by GREEN & SMITH—Executive and Advertising office at 2370—7th Ave., New York City, N. Y.—Tel. EDgecombe 4-0663. Manuscripts submitted for publication should be sent to 2370—7th Avenue, New York, and must be accompanied by return postage. No liability can be assumed for loss or damage to manuscript, although every possible precaution will be taken.

Subscription: Twenty-five cents per copy.

Advertising:—For rates write to the publishers and the same will be sent.

Last forms close on April 15th. We reserve the right to reject any advertising which in our opinion does not conform to our standards.

Published by
GREEN & SMITH
2370 SEVENTH AVENUE
NEW YORK, N. Y.

Across the diaspora, Black people continue to face discrimination, xenophobia, and persecution at higher rates than any other racial group.

About I Love Black People

The I Love Black People movement has a digital vision for the original Green Book. A Black survival guide that empowers and protects members of the African diaspora as they navigate the globe. This movement recognizes that Black lives matter every day. Black lives matter whether we are at home, abroad, visiting or transplanting ourselves. Our movement recognizes Black sovereignty when we collectively protect each other.
Black lives are saved when we share relevant information about our own safe spaces with our community. Black lives are improved when we support businesses that treat us with dignity & respect.

Victor H. Green

Our mission is to use technology to protect Black people from racism & xenophobia, especially when they are most vulnerable, while traveling or in new environments. We envision a world where people of African descent can safely travel and live without the fear of targeted harm or injustice.

Using critical historical sources like The Negro Motorists Green Book series, we are defining for ourselves, what it means to allow safe passage for Black people across the globe.

Chapter 5: ILoveBlackPeople.com Online Black Survival Guide

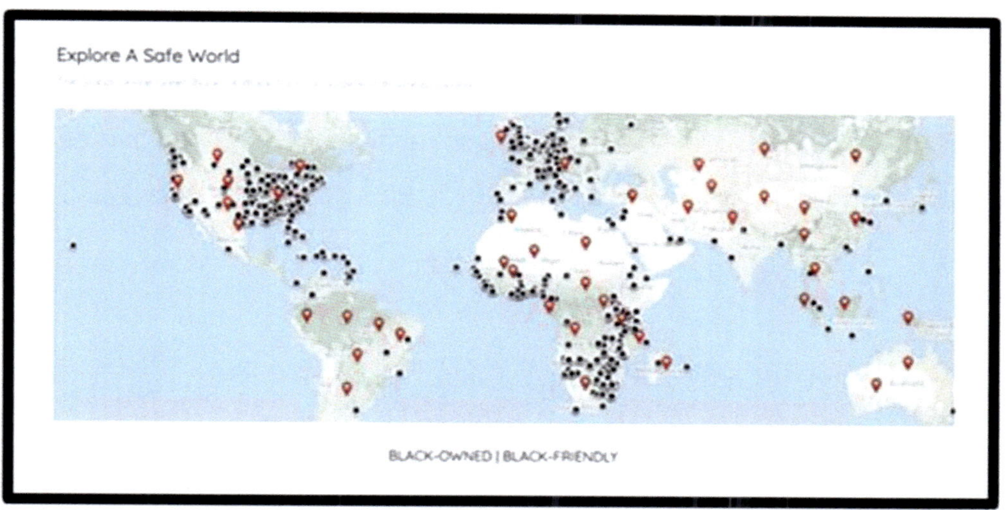

I Love Black People has expanded Mr. Green's vision and developed an online Global Green Book. ILoveBlackPeople.com is the essential digital survival guide built to help Black people avoid the harms and humiliations of racism.

ILoveBlackPeople.com is crowdsourced critical recommendations so that we can work together to protect and empower the African diaspora.

ILoveBlackPeople.com is a real-time interactive tool that searches Black-Owned and Black-Friendly businesses that prioritize protecting you from the harm & humiliation of racism and xenophobia.

ILoveBlackPeople.com

Visit online to:

SEARCH for Black Owned & Black Friendly businesses **RECOMMEND** Black Owned & Black Friendly businesses **JOIN** as a Free Member to protect Black people

JOIN as a Prime Member to Support the Movement

JOIN as a Founding Member to Contribute to the Movement **APPLY** to be a Brand Ambassador to Build the Community **ACCESS** Resources curated to Inform & Improve Black lives **ACCESS** our Media Library and Experience the Movement

ILoveBlackPeople.com Categories

1. **Accommodations:** Find the best hotels, Airbnb, hostels, and real estate agents.
2. **Health:** The best professionals in the fields of mental and physical health.
3. **Beauty:** Find hair salons, beauty supply stores, barbershops, beauty products, nail salons, and more.
4. **Food:** Restaurants, grocery stores, co-ops, food-trucks, catering companies, and more.
5. **Education and Childcare:** Find tutoring programs, home-schoo collectives, After School care- and summer camps.
6. **Legal:** Legal support.
7. **Finance:** Protecting our investments and planning the financial success of our families is critical. Find the best insurance agents, accountants, and financialservices.
8. **Transportation:** be it a rental, a place to getyour vehicle fixed o- a travel agent.

The Global Green Book API

The Global Green Book API is a B2B Essential Guide for Black people. It is meant to give access and engagement to I Love Black People's list of Essential Black-Friendly/Black-Owned businesses across the Globe for Non- Governmental Organizations, Governments and Corporations.
The District of Columbia has been the first government to provide ou- guide to its constituents. Find us at https://communityaffairs.dc.gov/moaaa

I Love Black People Ambassadors: Become An Ambassador

The mission of I Love Black People is accomplished primarily through our Brand Ambassador Program.

We are building a global movement to protect Black people from the harm & humiliation of racism & xenophobia, especially when they are most vulnerable while traveling and in a new environment. I Love Black People is inviting all brilliant people who pride themselves in disrupting Self- Hate in Our Communities.

Taking on a brand ambassador role means that we want you to represent I Love Black People with positivity and enthusiasm.

By doing so, you will help support Black people across the world.

Interested Persons Should:

- Have an appreciation of Pan Africanism
- Possess excellent communication skills and interact well in interdisciplinary and multicultural teams.
- Ability to work calmly under pressure with minimum or no supervisionand handling of multiple tasks
- Excellent creativity and confidence to share newideas.
- Go to iloveBlackpeople.com to APPLY today.

Brand Ambassador Responsibilities

- Disseminate our merchandise to large groups of people, especiallypositive social influencers with a large platform or following.

- Promote and get as many people as you know to become ambassadors and download the app.
- Wear our merchandise every time especially at predominantly Black social, political, and economic events.
- Develop creative and relevant social media content (i.e., posts and stories) that support the movement. (i.e., Making a story or post about your positive experience, with black-owned businesses or collegiate events).

Perks of being an ambassador?

- The opportunity to join a revolutionary movement. Supporting the cause of Anti-racism.
- Protecting Black people from the harm and humiliation of racismand xenophobia.

Go to iloveBlackpeople.com to APPLY today.

ILoveBlackPeople.com is focused on giving Black people the space to navigate the world while avoiding humiliation and harm caused byracism, xenophobia, and other forms of discrimination. We need your support to develop the most efficient and productive platform possible.

Chapter 6:
Year in Review: Newsletter Highlights

JUNE 29, 2021

I ❤ Black People

ILOVEBLACKPEOPLE.COM

A GLOBAL NETWORK TO HELP INFORM AND PROTECT BLACK PEOPLE

I ❤ BLACK PEOPLE

Somalia's First Female Taekwondo Athlete to Compete in Tokyo

Somalia has sent its first female taekwondo athlete to the summer games in Japan. No athlete representing Somalia has ever a won a medal at the Olympics, but 20-year-old Munirah Warsame is working hard to be the first. Warsame says flying the flag of her home country will be a proud moment.

FINANCE

DR Congo, Rwanda sign three agreements on bilateral cooperation

Rwandan President Paul Kagame met with his Congolese counterpart Felix Tshisekedi to sign agreements on Saturday, June 26. The agreements signed concern the promotion and protection of investments, the avoidance of double taxation and tax evasion between the two countries and gold mining cooperation. Security in the region, the eruption of the Nyiragongo volcano in May, and integration into the East African Community were also discussed. The two presidents have held many meetings in recent months, particularly during international summits.

EDUCATION AND CHILDCARE

Kenya, Burundi to prioritize education in post COVID recovery plans

Kenya President Uhuru Kenyatta and Burundi President Evariste Ndayishimiye recently signed several agreements aimed at strengthening cooperation between the two East African nations to strengthen and deepen their long-standing fraternal relations with the aim of fostering sustained socio-economic development. President Kenyatta announced a resolution by Kenya and Burundi to prioritize education in their post-Covid-19 recovery plans. The leaders have said they will continue working together in advancing the African agenda on the global stage, and reiterated their countries commitment to the progress of the East African Community.

LEARN MORE ABOUT I ❤ BLACK PEOPLE:

About Us | Membership | Shop | Become An Ambassador

LEGAL / PROTECTION

Guilty verdict in George Floyd's murder was an exception. Our work continues

As the former Minneapolis police officer was sentenced to 22.5 years in prison for the murder of George Floyd, Experts as the Center on Race, Inequality, and the Law at New York University School of Law assert that supporters of racial justice must not make the mistake of thinking that the verdict signals a fundamental change in the criminal legal system. Given the failure of so many other jurisdictions to hold officers accountable for abhorrent conduct, any sentence that didn't include significant prison time would likely have been met with understandable outrage. Prosecutors shifting the focus of this case from the police as whole to this officer as "one bad apple" underscores the problem of never meaningfully address the true source of the problem — namely, deeply rooted institutional racism and the legacy of slavery.

TRANSPORTATION

Black people are more likely to die in traffic accidents. Covid made it worse.

More Black people died in traffic deaths in 2020 than any other racial group even though Americans drove less in the pandemic. The number of Black people who died in such crashes was up 23 percent from 2019, the largest increase in traffic deaths among racial groups. Experts say this is not new and most likely represents another way the health crisis has had an outsize effect on Black people. Blacks are more likely to face traffic injuries and Black pedestrians were 82 percent more likely to be hit by drivers. Three major reasons are: infrastructure, design and racism. Predominantly Black neighborhoods are less likely to have crosswalks, warning signs and other safety mechanisms. And many high-speed highways are in or go through communities of color, as a result of federal effort in the 1950s to modernize the nation's roadways.

HEALTH AND WELLNESS

Cuba says Abdala vaccine 92.28% effective against coronavirus

In a measure of its efforts to be vaccine self-reliant, Cuba's health authorities announced their domestically produced Abdala vaccine has proven to be 92% effective against the coronavirus in clinical trials. This is the first COVID-19 vaccine to be developed in Latin America. And the perfect imagery for the story of a tiny island of 11 million inhabitants eager to show it can't be broken by a deadly virus and a 60-year economic blockade by the United States, and a country that boasts several brilliant scientists of its own.

The Black skin is not a badge of shame, but rather a glorious symbol of national greatness.

~ Marcus Garvey, founder and first President-General of the Universal Negro Improvement Association

ACCOMMODATION

The Algerian Revolution Changed the World for the Better

The legacy of the Algerian people and their liberation state is as dynamic, internationalist, and courageous as any in the world — the proud equal of a Cuba or a Vietnam in revolutionary heroics. Algerians had waged a long and furious struggle against colonization at its onset in the 1830s with little effect until the Sétif massacre in 1945 sent shock waves around the country, radicalizing the liberal independence movement. On November 1, 1954, the Algerian *Front de Libération Nationale* (FLN) declared war on France. Within the FLN camps, revolutionaries from across the African continent — including Nelson Mandela — received military and political training. Before they had even liberated their own homeland, the Algerians had already placed themselves at the center of pan-African and global Third World politics. The Algerian revolution was central to the political landscape of the mid-twentieth century and it remains one of the most modern states in the Arab world, both in terms of its infrastructure and culture.

BEAUTY

Aaraf Adam's Visual Project Spotlights Black Muslim Women in New Zealand

Twenty year old Sudanese-American artist, Aaraf Adam, is the founder of KanSuda, a new multimedia platform putting Black Muslim women and POC femmes on an overdue pedestal. Her new project entitled *Unity. Black Unity* aims to "empower and depict unity, love, and positivity for those who are underrepresented through visual art." As a Muslim woman who wears the hijab, Adam's faith is as much part of her identity as her race. She knows first-hand the damaging effects of Islamophobia and racism combined, reiterating the importance of her vision for her company. Adam hopes that her work inspires a new perspective.

FOOD

U.S. judge blocks $4 billion debt relief program for minority farmers

A U.S. federal judge has temporarily blocked a part of the federal stimulus relief package that forgave agricultural debts to farmers of color. A white farmer in Florida challenged the relief saying the debt relief program discriminated against him by race. The farmer is challenging Section 1005 of the American Rescue Plan Act, which provides debt relief to "socially disadvantaged farmers and ranchers." A separate judge in Wisconsin had also granted a temporary restraining order on the debt relief plan on June 10. The U.S. Agriculture Department (USDA) had planned to start the payments to farmers in June. For decades, USDA employees and programs have discriminated against socially disadvantaged farmers by denying loans and delaying payments, resulting in $120 billion in lost farmland value since 1920, according to a 2018 Tufts University analysis. Black farmers have been promised relief from federal discrimination in the past, only to be repeatedly disappointed. Eligible farmers are advised to continue paying on loans to avoid arrears if the program is permanently blocked.

SEPTEMBER 7, 2021

A GLOBAL NETWORK TO HELP INFORM AND PROTECT BLACK PEOPLE

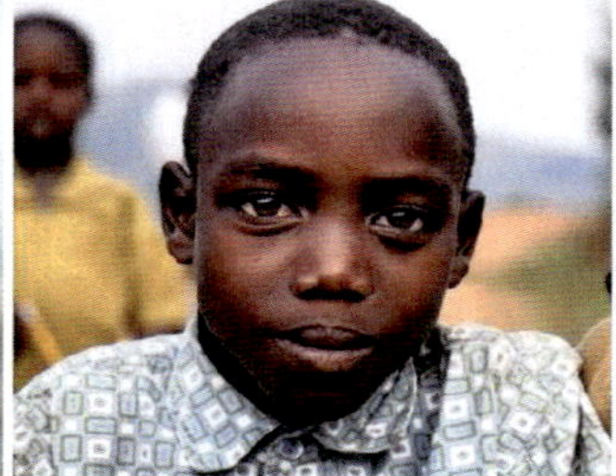

LEARN MORE ABOUT I ❤ BLACK PEOPLE:

About Us | Membership | Shop | Become An Ambassador

I ❤ BLACK PEOPLE

Rwanda: Video of Chinese employer beating local employee goes viral

From Sierra Leone to the DRC and now Rwanda, videos of Chinese managers viciously beating local employees is becoming a trend, with new clips appearing on social media channels every few weeks. The latest incident occurred in Rwanda's western Rutsiro province where a Chinese mining manager was caught on video whipping a local employee accused of stealing. The video shows the local employee tied to a pole with his hands bound and clearly showing signs of physical distress from the lashings. Although the clip was posted on The Chronicles newspaper's Twitter feed on Monday, it's not clear when the incident actually took place. Nonetheless, the video prompted authorities to take immediate action by arresting the Chinese national soon after the clip appeared online. Another interesting trend to watch is how quickly Chinese embassies in Africa are now responding. Until recently, Chinese embassies would only reluctantly respond, if at all, to these kinds of incidents. But in both Sierra Leone and now in Rwanda, the embassies promptly issued statements denouncing the violence within the same news cycle.

FINANCE

How this tech founder, an immigrant from Nigeria, is helping Americans save money and build credit

The Consumer Financial Protection Bureau reports that one in 10 Americans do not have credit history. The research further claims that about 26 million American adults have no histories with national credit reporting agencies such as Equifax, Experian and TransUnion. The study also finds that an additional 19 million have credit reports that are limited or out of date and unable to be scored. As a result, 45 million adult Americans do not have a credit score. Nigerian entrepreneur, Abbey Wemimo's background as an immigrant in America influenced the co-founding of Esusu Financial, a digital savings program. He first came to America from Nigeria in 2009 with his family. With few options, his mother had no choice but to accept a loan with a 400% interest rate so she could settle the family and also pay for Wemimo's college education. He notes that immigrants without credit histories are usually denied loans from traditional financial institutions. After obtaining a degree in business management and public administration, Wemimo decided to create a way for immigrants like him and low to medium-income earners in America to save money and establish credit.

TRANSPORTATION

Zimbabwe: New Beitbridge Freight Terminal Opens Next Month

The newly-upgraded commercial terminal, built under the US$300 million Beitbridge Border Post modernization project is set to open to commercial traffic on October 6. Southern African Development Community's busiest inland port of entry is being upgraded in three phases through a 17-year Built Operate and Transfer arrangement between the Government and Zimborders Consortium. Under the initiative, the Government is providing technical support while Zimborders, through various financial institutions, is funding civil works. The current border which handles at least 1 200 commercial heavy trucks, 3 500 light motor vehicles, 120 buses and 15,000 travelers daily is expected to carry five-fold its capacity upon full completion next year.

LEGAL / PROTECTION

The Enduring Legacy of Elijah McClain's Tragic Death

On August 24, 2019 Elijah McClain was walking home from a convenience store with iced tea for a younger sibling. McClain had been wearing a ski mask because his anemia made his body run cold; that he was likely dancing to music on his phone; that someone saw a man in a mask, moving unevenly in the street, and that the person phoned the police. The call led to a violent takedown of the young man, which led to the large dose of ketamine that was injected into his body and ultimately induced a series of heart attacks that ended his life a week later. In summer 2020, the nation's attention turned to the killing of the 23-year-old. As protests over racial justice raged across the country last year, thousands of people—from Hawaii to Maine—wrote letters and postcards to Colorado Gov. Jared Polis and demanded accountability for the death at the hands of Aurora police. While many of the letters might not have ever been opened, on September 1, Colorado Attorney General Phil Weiser announced that a statewide grand jury indicted two Aurora Police officers, one former officer, and two Aurora Fire Department paramedics in the 2019 death of Elijah McClain. Each of the defendants involved in McClain's death will face one charge of manslaughter and criminally negligent homicide, plus multiple assault charges.

> *You must never be fearful about what you are doing when it is right.*
>
> *~ Rosa Parks, American civil rights activist*

BEAUTY

5 Black Perfumers Changing the Scent Industry

Nielsen reported in 2018 that Black people were the biggest consumers of fragrance, responsible for 23 percent of the market (which translates to $151 million) while making up 14 percent of the population. Despite being such avid consumers of fragrance, Black people are rarely, if ever, represented in the industry — whether in advertisements, behind the scenes, or in retail spaces. Currently, Chris Collins, who helms the eponymous fragrance line World of Chris Collins, is the only Black perfumer in luxury retailers like Bergdorf Goodman and Nordstrom. But that doesn't mean Black talent is otherwise nonexistent in the space. Black perfumers do exist — as do reviewers and retailers — they're just few and far between. Five professionals shaking up the industry, share their career journeys, their hopes for change, and why diversifying the scent world is a priority. Maiya Nicole, Kimberly Walker, Dawn Marie West, Ezra Lloyd-Jackson and Kimberly Waters are five up and coming professionals to keep an eye on.

ACCOMMODATION

A Black-owned casino bets on a Black neighborhood in the former capital of the Confederacy

Alfred C. Liggins III, CEO of Silver Spring-based media conglomerate Urban One, plans to build One Casino and Resort with a 250-room hotel, a live theater, 1,800 slot machines and 100 table games in a long-neglected, majority-Black Richmond, Virginia area. The casino will bring $525 million in new tax revenue, 1,300 jobs paying at least $15 per hour and an influx of 3.7 million tourists annually to a city of just 227,000. Even as some community activists and political candidates hailed the casino, others denounce the project questioning if it will help improve the community. Read more to decide for yourself.

HEALTH AND WELLNESS

Discrimination Impacts Mental Health and Alcohol Use in Black Students

Black American college students are disproportionately affected by excessive alcohol use, and they are more likely to experience more negative social and health effects from drinking, compared to white peers. A new study linked problematic alcohol consumption to the depressive symptoms brought on by racial discrimination. The study found that participants who reflected positively about being Black had weaker connections between discrimination, mental health, and alcohol use. It also found that participants who felt good about being Black were buffered from the effects of how discrimination might impact their mental health and drinking behavior.

FOOD

How Eating Millet Can Cut Diabetes Risks

Millet is a fast-growing cereal plant that is widely grown in warm countries and regions with poor soils. It has gained popularity in the West because it's gluten-free and boasts high protein, fiber, and antioxidant contents. New studies show that a millet-based diet could lower the risk of diabetes, a rapidly growing problem in Sub-Saharan Africa. The study found that people with diabetes who consumed millets as part of their daily diet saw their blood glucose levels drop by 12-15%.

EDUCATION AND CHILDCARE

African languages to get more bespoke scientific terms

Many words common to science have never been written in African languages. Now, researchers from across Africa are changing that. A research project called Decolonise Science plans to translate 180 scientific papers from the AfricArXiv preprint server into 6 African languages: isiZulu and Northern Sotho from southern Africa; Hausa and Yoruba from West Africa; and Luganda and Amharic from East Africa. These languages are collectively spoken by around 98 million people. Earlier this month, AfricArXiv called for submissions from authors interested in having their papers considered for translation. The translated papers will span many disciplines of science, technology, engineering and mathematics. The project is being supported by the Lacuna Fund, a data-science funder for researchers in low- and middle-income countries. It was launched a year ago by philanthropic and government funders from Europe and North America, and Google. The Decolonise Science project is one of many initiatives that the group is undertaking; others include detecting hate speech in Nigeria and teaching machine-learning algorithms to recognize African names and places. The researchers hope to complete this project by the beginning of 2022.

I ♥ BLACK PEOPLE

AUGUST 24, 2021

A GLOBAL NETWORK TO HELP INFORM AND PROTECT BLACK PEOPLE

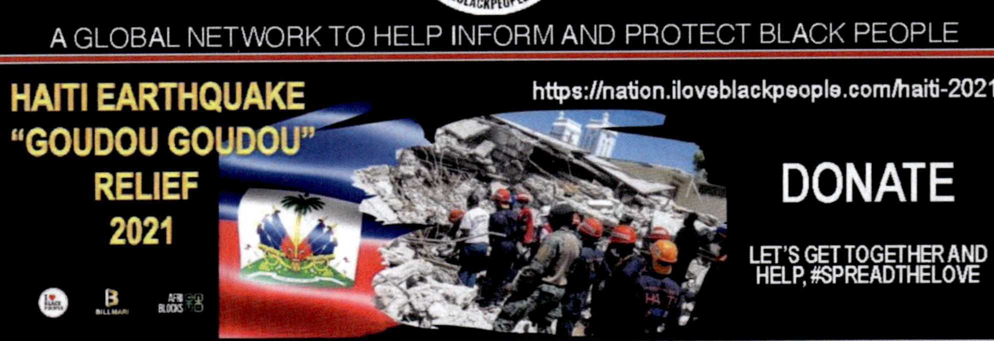

LEARN MORE ABOUT I ♥ BLACK PEOPLE:

About Us | Membership | Shop | Become An Ambassador

I ♥ BLACK PEOPLE

Memorial in Va. will honor first Africans brought to America

Fort Monroe will become the site of the African Landing Memorial, a space to honor the area where stolen Africans, arrived in English-speaking North America in 1619. The memorial, which aims to explore the significance of that moment in America's history is likely to be completed in the next few years. Already a national monument, Fort Monroe was named a UNESCO Slave Route Project site in February 2021. As a military installation, much of the fort's history pertained to its military operations, not necessarily the fort's place in history pertaining to slavery or the significance of the land on which it stands. The memorial will depict a series of events from 1619, when 20 Africans were ripped from their homeland in Angola, beginning hundreds of years of slavery. It will cover everything from the rich African culture left behind to the landing itself on the shores of America.

FINANCE

Minority communities are investing in crypto to escape financial discrimination

Black, Hispanic and LGBTQ Americans are significantly more likely to own crypto assets. According to surveys, 23% of Black Americans and 17% of Hispanic Americans indicated they are currently invested in digital assets, compared to only 11% of white Americans and 13% of the general public. Cryptocurrency awareness is also higher among minority groups, with half of Black Americans, Hispanic Americans and Asian Americans expressing familiarity with cryptocurrency, while only 37% of white Americans answered the same. The poll also found that 43% of Black Americans believe they have not been treated fairly by the banking and loans industries. By contrast, 28% of the general public said they had been treated unfairly by the finance sector.
Because many marginalized communities have experienced financial discrimination, it is likely contributing to their increased willingness to explore decentralized assets. CEOs suggest that Crypto is very big with Black millennials because it represents freedom as this is very much a social movement as representation and equality are what crypto promotes, evokes and distributes.

LEGAL / PROTECTION

Name Discrimination Study Finds Lakisha And Jamal Still Less Likely To Get Hired Than Emily And Greg

Economists sent 83,000 job applications to 108 Fortune 500 employers — half with traditionally white-sounding names, the other half with distinctively Black-sounding names. Applicants with Black names were called back 10% fewer times across the board — and even less when it came to specific companies — despite having comparable applications to their white counterparts. Researchers crafted resumes and automated the process of filling out employment history and personality tests. The study's authors used these names as a way of trying to understand discrimination in the employment application process. The study's authors have not yet followed up with the companies.

LEGAL / PROTECTION

Name Discrimination Study Finds Lakisha And Jamal Still Less Likely To Get Hired Than Emily And Greg

Economists sent 83,000 job applications to 108 Fortune 500 employers — half with traditionally white-sounding names, the other half with distinctively Black-sounding names. Applicants with Black names were called back 10% fewer times across the board — and even less when it came to specific companies — despite having comparable applications to their white counterparts. Researchers crafted resumes and automated the process of filling out employment history and personality tests. The study's authors used these names as a way of trying to understand discrimination in the employment application process. The study's authors have not yet followed up with the companies.

HEALTH AND WELLNESS

U.S. health spending 'disproportionately' tilted toward White people

The U.S. spends about 15% more on healthcare services for White people than for communities of color. Data from 2016 showed that of the roughly $2.4 trillion spent on healthcare for six common diseases, the most recent year for which data was available, 72% was allocated for White people. In comparison, 11% was spent on care for Black people, with the same percentage spent on Hispanic people. Black people account for just over 13% of the national population, while Hispanic people make up nearly 19%, according to figures from the 2020 census. This study focused on the care of more "routine" diseases, namely asthma, COPD, diabetes, heart disease, high blood pressure, low back and neck pain, and cerebrovascular diseases. Although Black people received approximately 26% less spending for care than the average for the total population, their costs for hospital and emergency-room services were 19% and 12% higher, respectively, than the national average.

ACCOMMODATION

New policy will mandate 'cheap homes' in some of Cape Town's most expensive areas

The Western Cape provincial government has developed a new draft housing policy aimed at addressing the province's 'legacy of apartheid spatial planning' and housing opportunity. The draft policy is based on multiple international case studies and will facilitate affordable housing in high-value locations. The policy intends to incentivize private developers to include affordable or social housing options in their respective market-driven developments. The policy will also allow cities or municipalities with developing property markets to form 'inclusionary housing overlay zones' in which affordable housing options can be encouraged or further developed on pre-existing properties.

> *"The ultimate measure of a man is not where he stands in moments of comfort and convenience, but where he stands at times of challenge and controversy."*
>
> *~ Dr. Martin Luther King, Jr., American minister and activist*

BEAUTY

The Persistent Joy of Black Mothers

Throughout generations, society has rendered Black mothers dangerous. The American mythology surrounding the so-called menace of the pathological Black matriarch of the 1960s, the treacherous welfare queen of the 1970s, and the drug-addled crack mother (and her babies) of the 1980s are alive and well. While white childbearing is generally thought to be a beneficial activity: it brings personal joy and allows the nation to flourish, Black mothers, however, are seen as harmful degenerates and a drain on the nation—a group to be controlled and disciplines --- even within Black communities themselves. Black mothers' private lives are consistently subjected to public surveillance, scrutiny, and judgment, as if to suggest that these women cannot be trusted to be responsible for themselves, or that they are unfit for motherhood. Recently, social-justice movements have helped expand and shift ideas about Black mothers and motherhood for the better, most notably through increased attention to the Black maternal-health crisis and through the advocacy of Black mothers who have lost children to police violence. Yet much of the American public still understands Black motherhood as an idea rooted in crisis. The Black mother as a figure, exists as a kind of public symbol, synonymous with pain. In classifying Black mothers as symbols of crisis, trauma, and grief, society robs them of their agency, flattening their complex identities. Merely seeing Black mothers as vessels, or symbols to be harnessed and deployed for political aims, denies a far richer understanding. As Black woman push against these ideals and troupes many are defining freedom for Black mothers as walking through the world living and thriving, without bracing for the trauma that results from white supremacy and rampant inequality.

TRANSPORTATION

South Africa's national infrastructure plan (NIP) open for comment

The draft plan was published for public review on August 10; written comments can be submitted until September 17. The NIP envisages an initial focus on delivering critical energy, transport, water and digital communications infrastructure development by 2050 and is linked to the national development plan (NDP), which is critical to long-term economic and social objectives. The NDP's objectives are focused on eliminating poverty and reducing inequality through various sectors, including infrastructure, to achieve, amongst others, an inclusive economy, building capabilities and enhancing the capacity of the state.

FOOD

Zimbabwean Young Farmers Lead the Charge in Agriculture

Agriculture in the country is on an upswing and young people are the driving force. Zimbabwe is set to harvest 2.8 million tons of maize this year, triple the 2020 harvest, making it the highest output in 20 years. The anticipated harvest should ensure food surplus. About 57% of Zimbabwean women ages 20 - 31 and 47% of men in the same age bracket are growing fruits such as mangoes and involved in rearing livestock. The government's pro-farming mindset is anchored in a program called "Pfumvudza" (meaning "Master Farmers' Revolution") through which it provides financing subsidies to young farmers.

EDUCATION AND CHILDCARE

South Africa Government plans to scrap school holiday

The Department of Basic Education (DBE) plans to cancel the October holiday period for schools in South Africa to help make up for lost teaching time. Under the current 2021 school calendar, government school students are on holiday from October 1 - 11 October. Scrapping this holiday would give students an additional week of teaching time from. All schools reopened on 26 July as part of the country's move to an adjusted level 3 lockdown after a month-long level 4 lockdown.

JULY 6, 2021

A GLOBAL NETWORK TO HELP INFORM AND PROTECT BLACK PEOPLE

AFRICA INDEPENDENCE DAY OBSERVANCES

LEARN MORE ABOUT I ❤ BLACK PEOPLE:

About Us | Membership | Shop | Become An Ambassador

I ❤ BLACK PEOPLE

What I Told President Biden in Tulsa

President Joe Biden visited Oklahoma's historically Black Greenwood neighborhood on June 1, to commemorate the 100th anniversary of the Tulsa Race Massacre. No other U.S. President had visited the site of one of the worst eruptions of racial violence in U.S. history. Before Biden spoke, he privately met with Tiffany Crutcher, founder of the Terence Crutcher Foundation, and her father. They are descendants of the Tulsa Race Massacre. Crutcher told the President that Black Tulsans need help in the fight for respect, repair, and restitution. Tulsa survivors confronted racism in the United States in its most overt form: A white mob—empowered and joined by government authorities—chased Black Greenwood residents out of their homes, killing hundreds of their friends and family members along the way, and then burned the thriving Black enclave to the ground. The terror for Tiffany and her father doesn't stop there. In September 2016, her twin brother, Terence, was shot and killed by Tulsa police as he stood unarmed next to his vehicle in the middle of the street. He was forty years old, and his killer was allowed to remain in law enforcement. The U.S. Department of Justice investigated the killing but never filed charges, reflecting the federal government's systemic failure to hold killer cops accountable. No person or entity responsible for the massacre, including the city of Tulsa, has paid for the lives lost and the community destroyed. Even insurance companies and banks turned their backs on Black Greenwood residents and have ignored their obligations to this day.

FOOD

Malawi President Lazarus Chakwera advocates improved food systems

President Lazarus Chakwera asked African leaders to take a bold step and ensure improved food systems and food security for their people. In his virtual address ahead of the United Nations (UN) Food Systems Summit Dialogue for African leaders, Chakwera said there was a need to institute industrial policies, promote private investment and job growth in local non-farm sectors. This year's summit, scheduled set for July 25 to 28, seeks to generate significant action and measurable progress towards the attainment of Agenda 2030 Sustainable Development Goals (SDGs). Chakwera said the summit would help Malawi to contribute to the attainment of SDGs as well as the country's efforts to domesticate the African Union Agenda 2063.

ACCOMMODATION

Comoros plans 1,000 housing units for the three islands

As part of the recovery project developed in the aftermath of Cyclone Kenneth, which devastated the country April 24 – 25, 2019, and caused more than $185M USD damage. Comoros' Ministry of Land Use Planning, Town Planning and Land Transport is responsible for implementing this project. The reconstruction will focus on housing as well as public and private infrastructure in the areas affected by the cyclone.

FINANCE

South Sudan poised to realize Nile dam dream, says deputy foreign minister

South Sudan plans to build a major dam along the Nile river in a bid to provide cheap, reliable electricity and help prevent devastating floods. The project is part of the oil-revenue funded government's plan to fix its many challenges. South Sudan came into existence as a country a decade ago and are trying to restructure and develop a solid plan for how the country will progress and grow. Seasonal rain pounds South Sudan's 10 states for at least seven months of the year, sending massive cascades of water into the White Nile, while also causing damaging flooding; new plans will help mitigate this occurrence. South Sudan also has plans underway to seek foreign investment to help build the dam.

HEALTH AND WELLNESS

News about Racial Violence Harms Black People's Mental Health

A growing body of research has documented the detrimental effects of both interpersonal and structural racism. The U.S. Centers for Disease Control and Prevention notes that centuries of racism have had a profound and negative impact on the mental and physical health of people of color. Investigators found that experiencing racism can result in traumatic stress linked to negative mental health outcomes, such as depression, anger and low self-esteem. The American Public Health Association calls racism a social determinant of health akin to housing, education, and employment and a barrier to health equity. Another study recently published adds a new layer to an understanding of the pervasive health effects of racism, noting that widely publicized anti-Black violence negatively affects the mental health of many Black Americans even if they do not directly experience it. Researchers assessed that Black respondents reported more poor mental health days during the time when two or more of these events happened in the country. Legal decisions not to prosecute or convict the officers involved in the killings were most clearly associated with poor mental health days.

EDUCATION AND CHILDCARE

What Trainee Science Teachers in Ghana Know About Climate Change

Ghana is taking steps to combat climate changes and have put a national climate change policy in place. The country recognizes the need for a skilled workforce of climate scientists and well informed citizens, and are making changes to science education and putting special emphasis on training teachers. Ghana's basic and high school science curricula now include study of the greenhouse effect, climate change, and the causes and effects of ozone depletion. Elementary and secondary school teachers play a critical role in preparing the next generation of climate scientists and climate-literate citizens. Teacher knowledge has a direct impact on what students learn, so efforts to improve climate science literacy must include attention to the ideas held by teachers. Their understanding of the relationship between ozone depletion and global warming could have a lasting and far-reaching impact.

BEAUTY

Africans Are Full Of Aesthetics: The Danger Of A Stereotype

This article tackles how western media has portrayed Africa. Initially Africa was viewed as impoverished and disconnected from the experiences of the rest of the world. This constant misrepresentation began to draw criticism and did not comprehensively reflect the everyday positive experience of Africans in Africa. Now, in a bid to compensate for the earlier misrepresentation an overly artistic image of Africa as an alternative to the depleted image of Africa is still in itself a stereotype. The author challenges the world to think holistically of Africa. Africans are capable of more than creative expression and the media should recognize the many dimensions of the African mind – the African that has a strong sense of aesthetics, but also the African that can make complex intellectual decisions.

LEGAL / PROTECTION

Ohio police chief resigns after putting KKK sign on Black officer's desk

A police chief in Ohio resigned after he put a Klu Klux Klan (KKK) sign on a Black officer's desk. Surveillance footage of the incident was aired on a local television station. When the town mayor learned of the incident, he fired the police chief and apologized to the officer for the incident. The police chief said that the incident was "overblown."

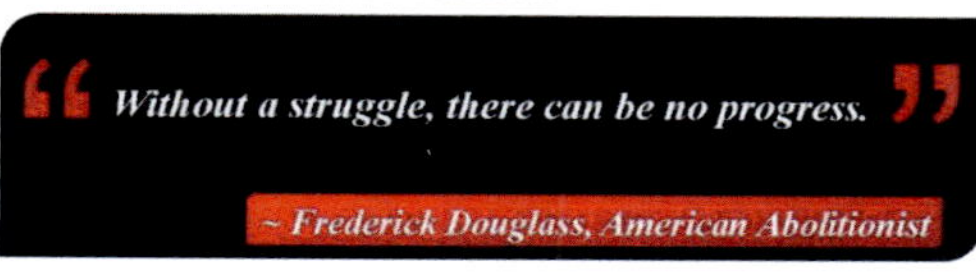

TRANSPORTATION

Asylum seekers face abuse, discrimination in Canada's immigration detention system

Human Rights Watch and Amnesty International say Canada detains thousands of asylum seekers in often abusive conditions. The two human rights organizations released a joint report on how people in immigration detention are regularly handcuffed, shackled and held with little to no contact with the outside world. Detainees who are from communities of color, particularly Black detainees, are held for longer periods, often in provincial jails. Canadian authorities are being called on to end the inhumane treatment of people in the system by gradually ending immigration detention in Canada. The Canada Border Services Agency remains the only major law enforcement agency in Canada without independent civilian oversight, which repeatedly resulted in serious human rights violations.

DECEMBER 7, 2021

A GLOBAL NETWORK TO HELP INFORM AND PROTECT BLACK PEOPLE

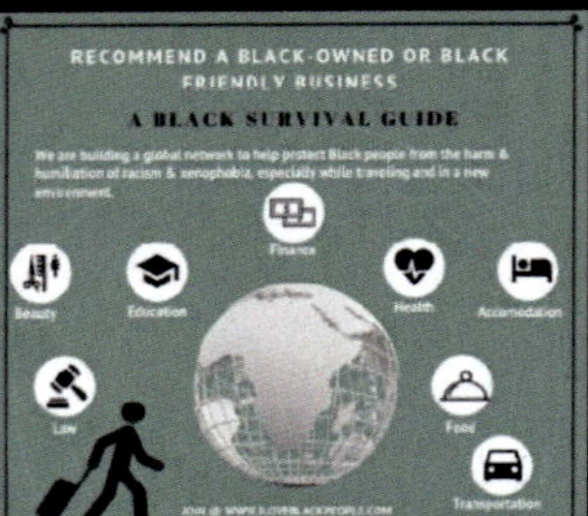

LEARN MORE ABOUT
I ❤ BLACK PEOPLE:

About Us | Membership | Shop | Become An Ambassador

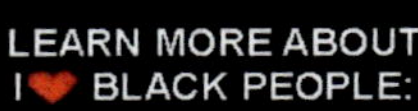

I ❤ BLACK PEOPLE

Factbox: The international campaign for slavery reparations

As Barbados dropped Britain's Queen Elizabeth as head of state, campaigners on the Caribbean island that received 600,000 enslaved Africans between 1627 and 1833 renewed their campaign for reparations. When Black slaves in the United States were freed after the Civil War, their families were promised up to 40 acres of land to help them survive economically. That promise was not kept. Over the years, reparations have been sought in the form of financial payments to the descendants of slaves, commitments to fund initiatives to help address economic disadvantages suffered by people of color in Western nations, and aid and debt forgiveness to African nations from which slaves were taken over the centuries. Calls for reparations have come from U.S. Black political leaders, many non-governmental organizations, religious groups including the Nation of Islam, Caricom, a grouping of Caribbean states, and nations including Nigeria. Individuals who said they were descendants of slaves have also initiated legal proceedings in the United States seeking reparations. While most focus has been on governments, lawsuits and public pressure have been brought to bear against companies and some individuals including the now collapsed investment bank Lehman Brothers, insurer Aetna Inc. and tobacco firm R.J. Reynolds, saying they or their corporate ancestors benefited from slavery.

TRANSPORTATION

African leaders condemn travel restrictions as omicron variant spreads globally

African leaders are pushing back on travel bans imposed by wealthy or Western nations in an effort to stop the spread of the highly transmissible omicron variant — and expressing their anger that the result of South Africa's openness in sharing news of the variant has led to what they see as punitive measures. The variant was detected in late November in Botswana and South Africa, and since then it's been found in countries across the globe from Scotland to Canada. It's still unclear where the latest known strain originated. Yet the travel restrictions specifically target nations in southern Africa. This prompted blowback from African leaders and public health officials, who say the bans will do more harm than good and discriminate against countries in the region. Several countries have taken steps to limit the flow of travelers from southern Africa. In the U.S., the Biden administration began restricting travel from eight nations. In the U.K., 10 countries were added to its "red list," a list of places the government defines as high risk for new and emerging strains of coronavirus. Canadian authorities have blocked foreign nationals who had recently been in seven countries from crossing its border. The European Union urged member states to limit travel from southern Africa, and Japan, Australia and Israel are banning all foreign travelers in response to the variant. The World Health Organization noted that only two of the countries on these lists — Botswana and South Africa — have reported cases. Yet other countries where the variant has been detected, such as the U.K., Canada and Germany, did not appear to be facing travel bans.

FINANCE

Netflix Invests $100M in Black-Led Banks to Help Narrow Racial Wealth Gap

Netflix said it has invested $100 million so far into six Black-led financial institutions in the U.S., as part of the company's pledge to allocate 2% of cash holdings into banks serving Black communities. Netflix announced plans to invest capital in Black banks to help address racial wealth inequality in June 2020. As of Sept. 30, 2021, the company reported $7.5 billion in cash and equivalents on its balance. Because the streamer pegged its commitment to 2% of cash reserves, the investment is anticipated to grow over time: At the end of 2021, Netflix plans to top up the funding and put more cash into the financial institutions.

LEGAL

What true justice for Ahmaud Arbery (and many others) would look like

When the jury returned guilty verdicts for the three men who murdered Ahmaud Arbery, there was a collective sense of relief; justice had been done. But it almost didn't happen; and in too many other cases, it never happens at all. Each of the defendants on trial for Arbery's murder was accused of multiple murder charges based on different sets of facts and provisions of Georgia law. Justice was possible here because there was videotape of the crime in progress. But, casting a wider lens, it's impossible to escape the conclusion that our system doesn't always achieve justice. We cannot rest on the verdicts in Arbery's murder as a sign that justice has come to Georgia, or to the deep south, or to our country. Because it hasn't. There is still so much work to be done. Read more as the author provides insights on the not yet passed, George Floyd criminal justice reform bill, unaddressed qualified immunity, and the nightmare conditions inside U.S. prisons as well as the criminal justice system, and over-policing in poor communities. The author reminds us that while justice ultimately came for Mr. Arbery, it came too late. It should have come while he was still alive. It should have come without the need to indict a prosecutor who delayed it and it shouldn't have taken publication of a video for law enforcement to treat the death as a crime. It should have come as part of a transformation of our society that permitted us, instead of politicizing critical race theory, to understand and confront our shortcomings though the lens of the racial injustice that permeates American history.

BEAUTY

Why Is Black Men's Skin Still Being Ignored by the Beauty Industry?

It is no longer an industry secret that Black skin has been marginalized. And while action has been taken for greater representation in the mainstream beauty industry, there is still an overwhelming disconnect we are left to face, namely, how Black men's skin is being seen and treated. Largely ignored and often misunderstood, we asked brand founders and dermatologists what can be done to change the existing narrative surrounding Black men and the grooming industry. The global men's grooming market is worth $70 billion, and unfortunately, Black men's needs and concerns are largely glossed over when it comes to marketing, branding, and exposure. Traditionally, men have been positioned as individuals that need to provide and look after the family. Expected to carry out the ideals of masculinity, only the grooming basics such as brushing/combing your hair and washing your face have been taught to them. The tables are turning, however, with society placing greater importance on health and wellness, and men are seeking the time they need to integrate grooming habits. Still, with this new narrative, Black men are finding it difficult to enter the grooming space when brands are not investing in representation and market education, which encourages an endless and tiring cycle. Inclusion, education, and support will be key in these things not happening in the future. But for all of those three things to happen correctly, Black people — especially men — need to be involved in the conversation and, better yet, there needs to be more representation at the table where these decisions are made. With education and training comes awareness and acknowledgement, and with awareness and acknowledgement comes the ability to change and address the concerns for Black men.

FOOD

The African migrants running a food bank in Sicily

A group of Nigerian women are frantically preparing to open a food bank for African migrant families. It is organized monthly by Osas Egbon to assist those unable to feed themselves because of the Covid-19 pandemic. The initiative is part of work undertaken by the Women of Benin City, a group Egbon founded in 2015 with other women who were victims of trafficking to Italy. Each month the food banks gets up to 40 families who depend on these vital parcels, which include essential items such as oil, pasta, rice and tinned foods such as beef and tomatoes. Demand has surged since then as many people have lost their jobs and sources of income. About 33% of the 187,000 foreigners registered in Sicily two years ago were from Africa - but there are many thousands more who are unofficial and living in Palermo, which has a population of about 1.3 million. The food bank is run on a voluntary basis and Egbon uses her contacts with churches and local businesses for collections.

> *The most dangerous creation of any society is the man who has nothing to lose.* ”
>
> *~ James Baldwin, American writer and activist*

ACCOMMODATION

Detroit teacher and youth restoring Idlewild, the historical vacation spot for Black people

Maria Lawton Adams was inspired to restore Idlewild, a historical vacation spot for Black Americans, after a tour of the remains in the summer of 2020. She used to visit Idlewild with her family as a child. The small 2,700-acre community, built by four white couples in 1912, was made to be a vacation destination for Black people. During the '20s and '30s, many Black performers went there to perform safely due to rampant racism and segregation of the time. Acts like Della Reese, Dizzy Gillespie, the Four Tops, and even Aretha Franklin performed there. By the '50s and '60s, Idlewild was a thriving hub for Black entertainers and families from across the country. Decades later, the forgotten town was left abandoned and in need of major renovations. Lawton Adams became inspired to get the youth in Detroit involved in transforming Idlewild back into the lively town it once was. Youth suffering through the lockdown could also build skills while giving back to the community. Lawton Adams has 25 kids involved in helping restore the community.

HEALTH

Grant Hill teams with Dendreon Pharmaceuticals to raise awareness on Black men And prostate cancer

Prostate cancer is killing Black men and the numbers are staggering. Not only is it the most commonly diagnosed cancer for African American men, but they're two times more likely to be diagnosed with and two and a half times more likely to die from prostate cancer. African American men also tend to develop prostate cancer at a younger age, have a more advanced form of the disease when found and are likely to have a more aggressive type of prostate cancer. This is the second-leading cause of death in African American men. Former five time All-NBA player, Grant Hill has partnered with Dendreon Pharmaceuticals and Dr. Michael Bivins of the Urology Centers of Alabama for the Start Strong campaign to encourage African American men living with prostate cancer to get screened early and take control of their health by developing a treatment game plan with their doctor. One issue that may have been scaring Black men away from getting tested in the past is the was an invasive test that was used. Today, the screening for prostate cancer is a simple blood test.

EDUCATION AND CHILDCARE

Dismantling anti-Black racism in our schools: Accountability measures are key

While Canada is known for its excellent education, this reputation can hide the realities of its Black students. With ample data demonstrating the effects of systems that undermine educational opportunities of Black students, it's clear that access to education in Canada isn't equitable and inclusive. Read more about how the Toronto District School Board's (TDSB) Centre of Excellence for Black Student Achievement offers a way to improve with a new targeted approach to addressing anti-Blackness. The centre offers a model based on strategic community engagement that school boards across Canada can learn from and enact. The Centre aims to develop an education system where anti-Blackness is dismantled with targeted anti-racist policy and practice. This involves introducing accountability measures to counter the full spectrum of educators' discriminatory practices that devalue Black life.

Chapter 7: Global Survival Guide Index: Africa Selected Countries & Airports

Accommodation, Food, Transportation, Health, Legal, Beauty, Education, Finance

Go to iloveBlackpeople.com to Recommend Now

AMERICA - NORTH AMERICA

Accommodation. Food. Transportation. Health. Legal. Beauty. Education. Finance

---

Antigua and Barbuda

St

The Bahamas

Nassau

Barbados

Bridgetown

Belize

Belmopan

Canada

Toronto
Costa Rica
San Jose

Cuba

Havana

Dominica

Roseau

Dominican Republic

El Salvador

San Salvador
Grenada

Saint George's

Guatemala

Guatemala City

Haiti

Port-au-Prince

Domingo

Jamaica

Kingston

Mexico

Mexico City

Panama City

Saint Kitts

Basseterre

Saint Lucia

Castries Montreal
Saint Vincent and the Grenadines

Kingstown

Trinidad and Tobago

Port of Spain

Santo

Honduras Tegucigalpa

United States of America

Alabama
Montgomery

Alaska
Anchorage
Juneau
Arizona
Phoenix

Arkansas
Little Rock

California
Los Angeles
San Francisco
Sacramento
San Diego
San Jose

Colorado
Denver

Connecticut
Hartford
Delaware
Dover

District Of Colum-Bia
Washington DC
Maine
Augusta

New Jersey
Newark
Jersey City

Florida
Jacksonville
Miami
Tampa
Tallahassee
Orlando
Georgia
Atlanta

Hawaii
Honolulu

Idaho
Boise

Illinois
Chicago
Springfield

Indiana
Indianapolis

Iowa
Des Moines
Kansas
Topeka

Kentucky
Louisville
Frankfort
Louisiana
New Orleans
Baton Rouge

Maryland
Annapolis
Baltimore

Massachusetts
Boston
Michigan
Lansing
Detroit

Minnesota
Minneapolis
Saint Paul

Mississippi
Jackson

Missouri
Jefferson City
Kansas City
St. Louis

Montana
Helena
Nebraska
Omaha
Lincoln

Nevada
Carson City
New Hampshire
Concord

New Mexico
Albuquerque
Santa Fe

New York
New York
Albany

North Carolina
Charlotte
Raleigh
Greensboro
Durham
Winston Salem

North Dakota
Bismarck

Ohio
Columbus
Cleveland
Cincinnati
Toledo

Oklahoma
Oklahoma City

Oregon
Portland
Salem

Pennsylvania
Harrisburg
Philadelphia
Pittsburgh

Rhode Island
Providence

South Carolina
Columbia

South Dakota
Pierre

Tennessee
Nashville
Memphis

Texas
Houston
Dallas
Austin

Virginia
Richmond

Washington
Seattle
Olympia

Wisconsin
Cheyenne

AMERICA - SOUTH AMERICA

Accommodation. Food. Transportation. Health. Legal. Beauty. Education. Finance

---

Argentina
Buenos Aires

Bolivia La
Paz
Santa Cruz

Brazil
Sao
Paulo
Brasilia
Rio

Chile
Santiago

Colombia
Bogota
Cali
Medellin

Ecuador
Quito

Guyana
Georgetown

Paraguay
Asuncion

Peru
Lima

Seriname
Paramaribo

Uruguay
Montevideo

Venezuela
Caracas

EUROPE

Accommodation. Food. Transportation. Health. Legal. Beauty. Education. Finance

---

Albania

Tirana

Andorra
Andorra la Vella

Armenia
Yerevan

Austria
Vienna

Azerbaijan
Baku

Belgium
Brussels

Bosnia & Herzegovina
Sarajevo

Bulgaria
Sofia

Croatia
Zagreb

Cyprus
Nicosia

Czechia
Prague

Denmark
Copenhagen

Estonia
Tallinn

Finland
Helsinki

France
Paris

Georgia
Tbilisi

Germany
Berlin

Greece
Athens

Greenland
Nuuk

Hungary
Budapest

Iceland
Reykjavik

Ireland
Dublin

Italy
Rome
Mila

Kazakhstan
Nur-Sultan

Kosovo
Prishtina

Latvia

Riga

Liechtenstein

Vaduz

Lithuania

Vilnius

Luxembourg

Luxembourg

Malta

Valletta

Moldova

Chisinau

Monaco

Monte Carlo

Montenegro

Podgorica

Netherlands

Amsterdam

North Macedonia

Skopje

Norway

Oslo

Poland

Warsaw

Portugal

Lisbon

Romania

Bucharest

Russia

Moscow

San Mario

San Mario

Serbia

Belgrade

Slovakia

Bratislava

Slovenia

Ljubljana

Spain

Madrid

Barcelona

Sweden

Stockholm

Switzerland

City of Bern

Turkey

Istanbul

Ukraine

United Kingdom

London

Manchester

Vatican City

AUSTRALIA

Accommodation. Food. Transportation. Health. Legal. Beauty. Education. Finance

Australia Sydney Melbourne Perth Vienna

Go to iloveBlackpeople.com to Recommend Now

ASIA

Accommodation. Food. Transportation. Health. Legal. Beauty. Education. Finance

Bangladesh
Dhaka

China Beijing Shanghai

India Mumbai Delhi Bangalore

Indonesia Jakarta Iran Tehran

Israel
Tel Aviv

Japan Tokyo Osaka Hiroshima

Lebanon
Beiru

Malaysia Kuala Lumpur

Myanmar
Yangon

Malaysia
Kuala Lumpur

Myanmar
Yangon

Russia
Moscow
St Petersburg

Saudi Arabia
Mecca
Riyadh

South Korea
Seoul

Thailand
Bangkok

Turkey
Istanbul
Ankara

United Arab Emirates (UAE)
Dubai

ASIA

Accommodation. Food. Transportation. Health. Legal. Beauty. Education. Finance

To recommend visit iloveblackpeople.com

Algeria

The Martyrs-Memorial

Inspired by the Azadi Tower in Tehran, this iconic concrete monument was built to commemorate the Algerian War of Independence.

Algeria, also known as the People's Democratic Republic of Algeria, is North Africa's largest nation which borders the Mediterranean Sea. Algeria declared its independence from France in 1962, after a long protracted armed struggle. Algeria's population is comprised of Arab- Berber ancestry, the dominant languages being Algerian Arabic, Berber and French which is typically used by government and media outlets. The nation's capital is Algiers, and the nation as a whole is 97% Muslim. This large North African country is said to have the highest estimated cost of living inthe region where they use the Dinar. Most of the population is concentrated along the Mediterranean Sea, which is a major site of tourism itself. Steeped in its revolutionary history one of Algeria' attractions is Martyrs' Memorial, which is a monument built to commemorate the nations' independence.

Angola

Huambo-Luanda

The Kifangondo Memorial was built to honor the memories of those who fought in the battle of Kifangondo. Just before Angola's Independence, anti-communist rebels supported by Portugal, South Africa and Zaire tried to occupy Luanda with less than a day to the declaration of independence and hand over of power by Portugal.

Angola, located on the Southwest Atlantic coast of Africa, declared its independence from Portugal after over a decade of armed struggle. The nation is well positioned sharing borders with Namibia, Zambia and the Democratic Republic of the Congo. Angola is well known as the origin of many Diasporic African populations in the Americas. The nation's population is primarily Ovimbundu, Ambundu, Bakongo the dominant languages are Bantu and Portuguese.

Angola's strength is its natural wonders and sites; namely, The Tundavala Fissure that can be found between the cities of Lubango and Namibe at an elevation of 2,600m above sea level, an ideal

location for hikers and sightseers. Next, situated in Lunda Sol, the Dala Waterfalls are about 60m high and conjure a stunning scene. Not far from Dala, is the site of another waterfall, Cassengo Falls. The Arch Lagoon is located in the Namib Desert not far from the town of Tombwa which is another natural site. The lagoon takes its name from the stunning natural arch rock formations that have been shaped by the elements over many years. Finally, in the province of Malanje there are the Black Stones of Pungo Adongo; another set of natural rock formations thought have formed over at least millions of years ago.

The Kifangondo Memorial was built to honor the memories of those who fought in the battle of Kifangondo. Just before Angola's Independence, anti-communist rebels supported by Portugal, South Africa and Zaire tried to occupy Luanda with less than a day to the declaration of independence and hand over of power by Portugal.

Botswana

Gaborone-The Three Dikgosi Monuments:

The Three Dikgosi Monument is a bronze sculpture located in the Central Business District of Gaborone, Botswana. The statues depict three dikgosi (tribal chiefs): Khama III of theBangwato, Sebele I of the Bakwena, and Bathoen I of the Bangwaketse.

Home of the world's oldest population the Khoisan people, Botswana is located in the interior of southern Africa. The nation is insulated by Zambia in the north, Zimbabwe to the east, south Africato the south and Namibia on the west. This area of south-ern Africa has been inhabited for a hundred thousand years, in the last century there has been regional integration and migration in the area by those inhabiting the Great Zimbabwe empire which stretched into Botswana. Today, the dominant ethnic groups are the Botswana, Tswana, Kalanga andBasarwa

Some of the main attractions in Botswana are Tsodilo Hills, an ancient sacred site with over 4,000 rock paintings created by the

Khoisan people who have inhabited the region for at least 100 thousand years. The Khoisan believe this to be the birthplace of humanity. Another must see is, Matsieng's Footprints & the Cradle of Humankind, Bahurutshe Cultural Villages in Gaborone, as well as the Three Dikgosi (Chiefs) Monument dedicated to the liberation of Botswana in 1966.

Seretse Khama International Airport - Botswana

Seretse Khama international Airport Sir Seretse Khama

Sir Seretse Khama International Airport, located 15 kilometers north of downtown Gaborone, is the main international airport of the capital city of Botswana. The airport is named after Sir Seretse Khama, the first president of Botswana. Seretse Khama was born in 1921 in Serowe, in what was then the Bechuanaland Protector- ate. He was the son of Queen Tebcgo and Sekgoma Khama II, the paramount chief of the Bamangwato people, and the grandson of the king, Khama III. The name "Seretse" means “the clay that binds" He was named this to celebrate the recent reconciliation of his father and grandfather; this reconciliation assured Seretse's own ascension to the throne with his aged father's death in 1925. At the age of 4, Seretse became kgosi (king), with his uncle Tshekedi Khama as his regent and guardian.

He became involved in local politics, being elected to the tribal council in 1957 as its secretary. In the 1961 Birthday Honors, he was recognized for his services as a tribal secretary by his appointment as an Officer of the Order of the British Empire (OBE). In 1961, Khama returned to politics by founding the Bechuanaland Democratic Party. As Prime Minister of Bechuanaland, Khama continued to push for Botswana's independence while based in the newly established capital of Gaborone. A 1965 constitution delineated a new Botswana government, and on 30 September 1966, Botswana gained its independence.

At the time of its independence in 1966, Botswana was the world's third poorest country, poorer than most other African countries. Its infrastructure was minimal, with only 12 kilometers 7.5 miles) of paved roads; and few of its people had a formal education, with only 22 university graduates and 100 secondary school graduates. Khama set out on a vigorous economic program intended to transform the nation into an export-based economy, built around beef, copper, and diamonds.

Khama instituted strong measures against corruption,

the bane of so many other newly independent African nations. The small public service was transformed into an efficient and relatively corruption-free bureaucracy with workers hired based on merit. Between 1960 and 1980 Botswana had the fastest growing economy in the world. Unlike other countries in Africa, his administration adopted market-friendly policies to foster economic development.

Burkina Faso

Ouagadougou

Monuments des Martyrs, located in Ouagadougou, the capital city of Burkina Faso, is most certainly one of the country's most unique structures. Also known as the Monument to National Heroes, it was one of the grand projects of the President of Burkina Faso in 1987 but ground was not broken until 2002.

This tiny West African nation shares borders with Mali, Côte d'Ivoire, Benin Togo and Ghana. Part of the Sahel, the capital of Burkina Faso is Ouagadougou. Burkina Faso was colonized by the French and is the home of esteemed revolutionary and Pan Africanist, Thomas Sankara. A multi-ethnic country with almost 30 ethnic groups, the majority being Mossi, the Fulani, Bobo, Gurma, Menda Senufo, Gurunsi, Lobi, Taureg, Soninke and Zarma.

Tiebele is a small traditional village located right next to the Burkina Faso/Ghana border. The Kassena people of Africa, one of the oldest ethnic groups of the country, originate from this village.

This village is an aesthetic wonder with its beautifully decorated mud huts and architecture. The Ruins of Loropeni, thought to be at least 1000 years old. Banfora is situated in one of the most beautiful regions of Burkina Faso, the Comoe Province it's appeal is the Tengrela Lake, and the KarfiguelaWaterfalls.

Thomas Sankara International Airport - Burkina Faso

Thomas Sankara International Airport President Thomas Isidore Noël Sankara

Thomas Sankara International Airport is an airport in the center of the capital city of Ouagadougou in Burkina Faso. The airport was named after the great Thomas Sankara of Burkina Faso. Thomas Isidore Noël Sankara was a Burkinabé military officer and socialist revolutionary who served as the President of Burkina Faso from 1983 to 1987. He was viewed by supporters as a charismatic and iconic figure of revolution and is referred to as "Africa's Che Guevara. At the age of 33, Sankara became the President of the Republic of Upper Volta. He named the country Burkina Faso, meaning 'Land of Upright People' from its colonial name, Upper Volta.

Here are some of the amazing facts about Africa's most celebrated icon, Thomas Sankara:

- Upon seizing power, he immediately sold off the government's fleet of Mercedes cars, replacing them with the ordinary Renault 5, the cheapest car in Burkina Faso. He reduced the salaries of all public servants and forbade the use of government chauffeurs and 1st class airline tickets. His own salary was only $450.
- He banned foreign aid to his country, arguing it was a means by the West to control poor nations. He reclaimed land from the feudal landlords and distributed it directly to the peasants. Wheat production in the country rose in three years from 1700 kg per hectare to 3800 kg per hectare, making the country food self- sufficient.
- He outlawed female genital mutilation, forced marriages, and
- polygamy in support of Women'srights.
- He also appointed women to high governmental positions, encouraged them to work, recruited them into the military, and granted pregnancy leave during education.
- He vaccinated 2.5 million children against meningitis, yellow fever, and measles in a matter of weeks.
- He planted over 10 million trees to halt the growing desertification of the Sahel.
- He declined to have his portrait hung in public places and government offices arguing that there were millions of Sankara's out there referring to his citizens.
- He was a strong campaigner for the unity of Africa.

Heartbreakingly, he was assassinated in a military coup led by his friend, Blaise Compaoré. Thirty years after he left, and the name Thomas Sankara is still stuck on almost every African's lips; his ideas are a cornerstone for all Pan-Africanists and his lasting legacy is celebrated not in Africa alone, but the world at large.

Burundi

Gitega

The Mausoleum of Prince Louis Rwagasore was built in 1961 after the death of the national hero, Prince Louis Rwagasore murdered October 13, 1961. It comprises a block with inscriptions of the National Currency: Ubumwe Ibikorwa Amajambere which means Unity, Work, Progress.

Burundi, formally known as the Republic of Burundi, is a small African nation in the interior of the African continent. It shares borders with Rwanda, Tanzania and the Democratic Republic of the Congo. Burundi is historically an agricultural society comprised of three primary ethnic groups, the Hutu, Tutsi and Twa. The dominant language is Kirundi, spoken by 98%. Burundi is one of the few African countries where one indigenous language has been adopted by the majority of the population. Establishing its independence in July 1962 from Germany, ironically, French is the western language utilized by the government and municipalities. The main attractions in Burundi are Gitega, Burundi's central plains which is the mountaintop of the Congo Nile Range. Lake Tanganyika is a major natural site and the Musee Vivant a display of Burundi's traditional culture is another must see.

Cameroon

Douala Yaounde

Located near the general area of Yaounde this monument was built in 1974, symbolizes the entire history of cameroon. Part of West Africa, Cameroon sits on the Atlantic coast and shares borders with Nigeria, Chad, the Central African Republic to the east, and Equatorial Guinea, Gabon and the Republic of the Congo in the south. Historically and ethnically diverse region, and then nation. Initially inhabited by the Baka, then Bantu groups, today the dominant ethnic groups are the Bamileke, Bamoun, Bassa, Douala, Ewondo, Bulu, Fang, Makaa and Fula or Fulani which span several nations. Cameroonians speak a number of Bantu- Sudanic languages. The national language is both French andEnglish.

Yaounde is the capital, but Douala is said to be the “economic capital”. Douala, which is a great city to visit, has numerous tea, banana, rubber and pineapple plantations. There are several traditional villages to visit in Lolodorf, Boumnyebel, Eseke as well as Bipindi in the forest.

Cape Verde

Cape Verde was discovered in 1456 by Portuguese mariners. Theislands were uninhabited but fertile enough to sustain settlers and agriculture. The land was literally built by Africanslaves

which these settlers enslaved and shipped from the West African Coast. However, after failing to use the land for agriculture, the settlers began to use the strategically positioned island for transatlantic slave trade.

Amílcar Cabral Monument

Within a century, the islands hadgrown wealthy enough to attract pirates, including a 1585 raid by England's Sir Francis Drake. In 1747, the changing weather patterns resulted in the island's first recorded drought. Inthe 00000 people – more than 40% of the population alism simmering on the mainland, established a uinea- Bissau, in 1956 Cape Verdean intellectual Amílcar Cabral (born in Guinea- Bissau) foun ded the Marxist-inspired Partido Africano da Independência daGuiné e Cabo Verde (PAIGC), later renamed the Partido Africano da Independência de Cabo Verde (PAICV). As most European powers released their colonies, the Portuguese dictator, António de Sala-zar held onto Cape Verdeand war ensued- one of Africa's longest wars of independence. Eventually, Portugal's war became an international scandal and led to the nonviolent demise of its dictatorship in 1974, with Cape Verde finally gaining full independence a year later.

Central African Republic

Memorial of the Revolution | Bangui

Chad

Ndjamena

Positioned almost directly in the center of northern Africa, sharing borders with Sudan, Central African Republic, Cameroon, Nigeria, and Niger in the west. Chad is comprised of many ethnic groups, The most dominant are the Sara, Kanembu, Budma, Arab, Masalit, Gorane, Massa, Musgium. Chad fought a long struggle for liberation, establishing their independence from the French in 1960. A major attraction in Chad is N'djamena, the capital. Next, Lake Chad, and then Douguia on the Chari River. Travelers to the country can take a canoe ride with local boatmen experiencing the daily life of local people.

Democratic Republic of the Congo (DRC)

Kinshasa Lubumbashi

Towering in the middle of a traffic circle in Kinshasa, Democratic Republic of the Congo, is a roughly 25-foot-tall statue of a bald headed, dour looking, Laurent Kabila, the former despotic leader of the DR Congo local boatmen experiencing the daily life of local people.

The Congo is arguably one of the most resource rich nations in Africa, if not the world. The home of national hero, freedom fighter and Pan Africanist Patrice Lumumba. Much of the Congo Free State is located in Central Africa insulated by the jungle. Pre-colonial Congo was comprised of three empires, Luba, Lunda and the Kongo. The Luba Empire was the largest and most dominant. The Congo was one of the last areas in this region to be colonized by European due to the dense jungle that protected the region from outsiders. Although seldom toured, places to visit in the Congo are the Congolese village of Makwatsha where a painting tradition has become an attraction. Other sites are, of course, the Congo River and Nkak. You can take a canoe to Nkake, Samba, Buya, and other traditional villages.

Abidjan

This West African country shares borders with Liberia, Guinea, Mali and Ghana. The ethnic composition of the Ivory Coast vast, comprised of over 60 ethnic groups. The majority being Akan, Baoulé, Gur, Mandes, Krou, and Bété. The Ivory Coast was colonized by the French and declared full independence in1960.

Where to go in Ivory Coast; First up, the city of Man, which yields plantain farms and cocoa plantations. Next, the peaks of Tonkoui and Toura, the two highest in Ivory Coast which dominate the horizon, this site also includes the Cascades waterfall which is a major attraction. If you're into beach life, there's Jacqueville which has ivory sand that leads to the Ebrié Lagoon, which has its own beaches. Finally, San-Pédro's which has many natural attractions, the Upper Guinean rainforests of the Taï National Park the beaches of Bas- Sassandra and Assouinde, a popular beach resort in the country. And finally, take a trip to the traditional village of Korhogo Village des Tisserands home to batik cloth makers.

Egypt

Cairo Alexandria

Tahrir Square, also known as "Martyr Square", is a major public town square in downtown Cairo, Egypt. The square has been the location and focus for political demonstrations in Cairo.

Egypt, the gem of the ancient world. Egypt occupies the northeast corner of the African continent, bordered by the Mediterranean in the north and the Red Sea to the east. ts regional neighbors are Libya and Sudan. The majority of the population today is identified as Egyptian with smaller groups in the region are Berbers, Siwa, and Nubians. A majority of the population speaks modern Egyptian– Arabic, smaller populations like Berbers, Nubians, Bedouins, and Copts also make up the demographic Egypt declared its independence from British unilateral rule in February of1922

Home of the famed and fertile Nile River Valley, there's a long list of sites to visit, namely the Pyramids at Giza, the Great Sphinx, Luxor's hieroglyph-lined temple located on the east bank of the Nile, Karnak Temple and the Valley of the Kings which holds 63 tombs. Don't leave the country without visiting Deir el Bahari the site of the Hatshepsut's Temple/ Mortuary, 18th Dynasty, on the west bank of the Nile, and the Bent Pyramid located at Dahshur, the second pyramid built by pharaoh Sneferu.

Ethiopia

Addis Ababa

Another gem of the ancient world, Ethiopia has much to offer. First off there's Addis Ababa the capital city, Ethiopia has a diverse population with over 80 ethnic groups. Majority of the population speak Afro-Asiatic languages, primarily of the Cushitic and Semitic branches. Ethiopia is one of only two African nations never colonized, the national language is Amharic. Ethiopia's regional neighborhoods are Eritrea, Djibouti, Somalia, Sudan, South Sudan andKenya

There's a list of must-see places to visit, a short list would include the Danakil Depression located between the Ethiopian and Eritrea border, the driest and hottest place on earth. Next up, the Rift Valley a string of lakes which includes the Hot Springs. The Blue Nile Falls on the Blue Nile. To engage indigenous life and people take a trip to the Lower Omo Valley to experience the Daasanach village. And finally, Aksum considered one of the oldest cities in all of Africa. Aksum, believed to be the home of the Queen of Sheba and the site of the sacred Ark of the Covenant.

Gambia

Banjul

Kunta Kinteh Memorial Statue

Ghana

Kumasi Accra

Eternal Flame of Liberation: This statue was built as a symbol of liberty & was first lit by Kwame Nkrumah, the first President of Ghana & the leader of Pan-Africanism.

Ghana is the African nation on the continent to declare its independence from the British in 1957 and home of Pan Africanist and Revolutionary, Kwame Nkrumah. Ghana, officially the Republic of Ghana is located along the Gulf of Guinea and Atlantic Ocean, is a destination favorite for travelers from the African Diaspora in the Americas. Its regional neighbors are Togo, Burkina Faso and Côte d'Ivoire

The must-see sites are Cape Coast and Elmina Forts major points in the Trans- Atlantic Slave Trade that sit along the Atlantic coast. Nkrumah's monument marking the nations independence, the DuBois Center memorializing the work of
W.E.B. DuBois. The nation's capital, Accra and Kumasi have numerous markets offering you the opportunity to engage the people and support thelocaleconomy.

Guinea

Conakry

Located at a busy intersection in downtown Conakry is this monument celebrating Guinea's successful effort to liberate itself from French colonial domination (formerly part of French West Africa) in1958.

Guinea is a country in West Africa, bordered on the west by the Atlantic Ocean. Its regional neighbors are Guinea-Bissau, Senegal, Mali, Côte d'Ivoire, Liberia, and Sierra Leone. Guinea's national pride is evident, on October 2, 1958, Guinea gained its independence from the French. A statue of Samori Toure, located down- town Conakry is symbolic of the Guinean struggle for liberation from French imperialists. There are numerous ethnic groups and languages spoken in Guinea the dominant ones are Susu, Pular (Foulah, Peuhl) and Malinke. The national language is French.

Sandervalia quarter of Guinea's capital and the cultural center of Conakry, where the National Museum of Guinea is. Another major attraction is the Lady of Mali a giant statue of a woman carved out of granite just north Conakry, near the Malian border. Conakry itself is a place to explore, but if you're into beaches Ile de Roume and Kassa, are just a boat ride away from the capital. And the beaches of Cape Verga, on the Guinea coastline, north of Conakry are comparable to those of Madagascar and the Caribbean. If you're into hiking, a trip to Petteh Djiga gives you a view of Gambia and Senegal's rivers, and an opportunity to encounter the farming communities of the Mande people.

Kenya

Nairobi Mombasa

Uhuru Gardens is the largest memorial park in Kenya & home of Kenya's national monument.

Kenya home of the revolutionary and Pan Africanist Jomo Kenyatta sits in the northeast region of Africa, its neighbors are Ethiopian, Somalia, South Sudan, Tanzania and Uganda. Once a settler colony. Kenya fought an armed struggle against the British. The nation established it independence in 1963 and declared itself a republic in 1964. The nation is ethnically diverse with over 40 different groups, the Kikuyu which historically inhabited the Highlands, the Luhya, Luo, Kalenjin, Kamba, and Meru are the dominant ones. Although most Kenyans speak their ethnic language the national language isSwahili.

The capital Nairobi is a bustling city; however, you get the real feel for Kenya by visiting the traditional villages. The Maasai are an indigenous semi-nomadic group that lives in northern Kenya. In western Kenya, lies the Alego Nyangoma Kogelo village, ancestral home of U.S. President Barack Obama. To the south are the ruins of Swahili villages, Gede ruins and Maralal a frontier town, the home of the Samburu. And… finally there's Amboseli National Park, where you can view Mt. Kilimanjaro over in Tanzania.

Jomo Kenyatta International Airport - Kenya

Jomo Kenyatta International Airport President Jomo Kenyatta

The Jomo Kenyatta International airport is located in Nairobi, the Capital of Kenya, named after one of the country's most celebrated heroes. Jomo Kenyatta was a Kenyan anti-colonial activist and politician who governed Kenya as its Prime Minister from 1963 to 1964 and then as its first President from 1964 to his death in 1978. He was the country's first indigenous head of government. Cde Kenyatta played a significant role in the transformation of Kenya from a colony of the British Empire into an independent republic. Ideologically an African nationalist and conservative, he led the Kenya African National Union (KANU) party from 1961 until his death. Being a Pan-African and anti-colonialist, Cde Kenyatta organized the 1945 Pan- African Congress in Manchester. He returned to Kenya in 1946 and in 1947, was elected President of the Kenya African Union, through which he lobbied for independence from British colonial rule, attracting widespread indigenous support but animosity from white settlers. He has imprisoned for master-minding the anti-colonial Mau Mau Uprising. On his release, Kenyatta became President of KANU and led the party to victory in the 1963 general election. As Prime Minister, he oversaw the transition of the Kenya Colony into an independent republic, of which he became president in 1964. 90

Here are some of his major achievements:

He was vital in securing Kenya's independence from Britain as he worked closely together with the then-British Prime Minister Harold Macmillan to map out a strategy for Kenya's independence.

Resolutely fought to protect the interest of the Kikuyu people He was a part of the Kapenguria Six who were arrested for masterminding the Mau Mau Uprising as Kenyans protested against land seizures by the British.

He co-organized the Fifth Pan-African Congress (1945) where he vigilantly supported a resolution that called on European powers to immediately hand over the affairs of Africa to Africans.

Jomo Kenyatta would be the father to Kenya's 4th president, the currently sitting President Uhuru Kenyatta. Cde Jomo Kenyatta's glorious history and selfless efforts to free Kenya will always be engraved on the hearts of Kenyans and Africa at large.

Lesotho

Maseru Maseru

Formerly the British colony of Basutoland, declaring its independence from the British in 1966, Lesotho is a small African nation in southern Africa. It shares borders with South Africa, Swaziland, and Mozambique. The name of the country, "Lesotho" translates as "the land of the people who speak Sesotho". The indigenous population of Lesotho are the Khoisan or San people which inhabit most southern African nations.

Lesotho has unbelievable natural sites and well-preserved traditional villages. These are a few, in Maseru District, is a community of bamboo-topped thatch villages and huts called Semonkong one of the most interesting and widely visited places in the country.91

This village also includes the great Maletsunyane Falls. Second, is Katse Dam once the largest of its kind in Africa. Moteng Valley is a community which date back to the Stone Age. Another highlight is Leribe where you can engage authentic Basotho life. In Leribe you can visit the local marketplace, Leribe Craft Centerand much more. Next, Thaba Bosiu plateau which is a historic natural fortress of the Basotho tribe, where they waged the Basuto Wars against the Boers during the Basotho conflicts. Last, but not least, before leaving the country one must visitthe Ha Kome cave houses of Lesotho's Berea District. Carved directly from the rock faces of the surrounding mountains, they can be found hiding between the valleys close to the village of Mateka.

Liberia

Liberia Liberation Monument

Monrovia

One of only two African nations on the continent of Africa never colonized by Europeans. Liberia, meaning "Land of the Free" sits on the Atlantic Coast of Africa, sharing borders with Ivory Coast, Guinea and Sierra Leone. Liberia was the destination of African people in the

U.S. who had survived enslavement and were resettled in Africa. This American- Liberian population would draft the constitution and establish it as the Republic of Liberia in 1847. Liberia has maintained it freedom and resisted attempts of Euro- pean colonization over the last two centuries. 92

Liberia has around 20 indigenous African ethnic groups, some of which are Kpelle, Bassa, Gio,Kru, Grebo, Mandingo, Mano, Krahn, Gola, Gbandi, Loma, Kissi, and Bella. Most of ethnic groups speak their indigenous languages, while English is the national language. Luxor's hieroglyph-lined temple located on the east bank ofthe Nile, Karnak Temple and the Valley of the Kings which holds 63 tombs. Don't leave the country without visiting Deir el Bahari the site of the Hatshepsut's Temple/ Mortuary, 18th Dynasty, on the west bank of the Nile, and the Bent Pyramid located at Dahshur, the second pyramid built by pharaoh Snefe-ru.

The capital Monrovia is an active city; but Liberia's main attractions are its seaside beaches. A few to visit are Buchanan which is just south of Monrovia. Gbarnga, also on the coast has waterfalls and quaint guesthouses. Marshall another city on the coast has empty beaches, palm forest and mangrove and camping on the Liberian coast.

Libya

Tripol

The Martyrs' Square; known as Green Square under the Gaddafi government; Independence Square during the monarchy; and originally known as Piazza Italia is a downtown landmark at the bay in the city of Tripoli, Libya.

North Africa, bordered by the Mediterranean Sea to the north, shares borders with Egypt, Sudan, Chad, Niger, Algeria to the west, and Tunisia. sovereign state is made of three historical regions: Tripolitania, Fezzan and Cyrenaica. Libya is the fourth largest country in Africa. Native Libyans are primarily a mixture of Berbers and Arabs. Small Tuareg and Tebu tribal groups in south-ern Libya which are nomadic or semi nomadic. Both France and Italy held territories in Libya, gained it total liberation in 1947.

Places to visit in Libya are, Leptis Magna, Cyrene and Sabratha. Other popular sites include Ghadames and the Arch of Marcus Aurelius.

Madagascar

Antananarivo

Madagascar is uniquely located off the eastern coast of southern Africa, in the Indian Ocean. On the eastern side of the Mozambique Channel, the country is the fourth largest island in the world. The indigenous population of Madagascar is

Malagasy, which is comprised of at least 20 ethnic groups, most of which have different cultures, norms, and religious beliefs. The dominant ethnicity. Consistent with this fact, there are around twenty-two dialects of Malagasy some of which share commonalities with Bantu languages, Swahili, Arabic, English, and French. French became the national language as a result of the colonial period and Malagasy became secondary. Madagascar became fully independent in 1960.

Sites to see are, Ifaty and Mangily, fishing villages on the south- western edge of Madagascar island. Ambanja and Nosy-Be are two of Madagascar's best beaches. Toliara and Ibsalo National Park are sites to explore carved rock gorges and winding canyons as well as real life blooming oases. Ambohimanga also called Royal Hill, a part of the island nation's cultural identity, which was once the home of local kings.

Republic of Malawi

Lilongwe

The Memorial Tower

The Republic of Malawi is a landlocked country in southeastern Africa formerly known as Nyasaland. It is bordered by Zambia to the west, Tanzania to the north and northeast, and Mozambique surrounding on the east, south and southwest. Its capital is Lilon-gwe, which is also the country's largest city.

The name Malawi comes from the Maravi, an old name of the Chewa people who inhabit the area. The country is nicknamed "The Warm Heart of Africa" because of the friendliness of its people. The part of Africa now known as Malawi was settled by migrating Bantu groups around the 10th century. Centuries later in 1891 the area was colonized by the British. In 1953 Malawi, then known as Nyasaland, became a protectorate within the semi-independent Federation of Rhodesia and Nyasaland. In 1964 the protectorate over Nyasaland was ended and Nyasaland became an independent country under Queen Elizabeth II with the new name Malawi. Two years later it became a republic. Upon gaining independence it became a totalitarian one-party state under the presidency of Hastings Banda. Malawi now has a democratic, multi-par-ty government headed by an elected president, currently Lazarus Chakwera. 95

Lilongwe - Kamuzu International Airport - Malawi

Kamuzu International Airport President Hastings Kamuzu Banda

Kamuzu International Airport is an international airport serving Lilongwe, the capital city of Malawi. It is also known as Lilongwe International Airport. The airport was named after the country's former president, the late Hastings Kamuzu Banda. He was the Prime Minister and later President of Malawi from 1964–1994 (forthe first year of his rule as it achieved independence in 1964, Malawi was the British protectorate of Nyasaland). In 1966, the country became a republic, and he became president. He received his education at Wilberforce Institute, an African American AME college, now known as Central State University in Wilberforce, Ohio, in the USA. He also received his second medical degree at the University of Edinburgh in the United Kingdom. Afterward, he returned to Nyasaland to speak against colonialism and advocate independence from the United Kingdom. He was formally appointed Prime Minister of Nyasaland and led the country to independence in 1964. He made Malawi a one- party state under the Malawi Congress Party (MCP) and they declared him President for Life. He is known for improving the country's infrastructure, maintaining a good educational system, and supporting women's rights.

Mali

Bamako

Officially known as the Republic of Mali, sharing borders with Algeria, Mauritania, Senegal, Niger, Guinea, Ivory Coast and Burkina Faso. Mali is the eighth largest country on the continent of Africa, its capital is Bamako. Mali gained it independence from the French in June of 1960. The dominant ethnic group and language is Bambara who speak Bamana. The smaller ethnic groups are Fulani which span several nations, Dogon, and Tuareg. Agriculture is the dominant economic sector some of the major industries are cotton, cattle and camel herding, and fishing.

Home of the famous city Timbuktu, an ancient learning center. Unfortunately, recent conflicts may not allow this site to be accessible to visitors. Other places to go are Gao the heart of the Songhai Empire where one can experience the ancient character of Mali. The city has craft markets and houses the acclaimed Sahel Museum, and 15th- century sepulchers like the Askia Tomb like the great pyramids of Egypt.

Morocco

Casablanca-Fes-Marrakech

Morocco is a North African country that borders both the Atlantic Ocean and Mediterranean Sea. It shares borders with Algeria, Mauritania and Mali. The nation is ethnically diverse with a combination of Berber and Arabian influences. Colonized by both France and Spain, Morocco gained its independence in 1956.

Morocco has its own medina in Marrakesh, the sprawling quarters of the city offers entertainment in its Djemaa el-Fna square and souks (marketplaces) where you can buy ceramics, jewelry and metal lanterns. You can get a real feel for Morocco in Fes, by visiting the Fès el-Bali the historic heart of the city. A visit to Morocco wouldn't be complete without a trip to Casablanca, the country's largest city, which also has a medina (holy city) but with a modern twist. In Meknes, visit the National Archeological Museum and the Modern Art Museum.

Mozambique

Maputo

Mozambique is a southeast-ern African nation that shares borders with Tanzania, Zambia, Swaziland and South Africa. Colonized by the Portuguese, Mozambique would have a long and eventful armed struggle.

National heroes are Eduardo Mondlane and Samora Machel who lead FRELIMO until the nation declared its independence in 1975.

Mozambique is a multi-ethnic nation, comprised of the Makua, Tonga, Chokwe, Manyika and Sau, Shona, Tsonga,Swahili and the Makonde who can also be found in Tanzania. Bantu- speaking groups were the first to inhabit this region,

Swahili and then Arabs groups Workers Square Monument arrived later, settling along the f agriculturalists.

Places to go; First, the capital city Maputo which e Quirimbas Archipelago is a main attraction with a st

the Indian Ocean, perfect for beach goers and divers. The largest island is Bazaruto. The city of Tofo, has an Indian Ocean coastline with beaches and offshore marine parks. Lake Cahora Bassa extends from the Zambia border to the very heart of Tete Province in western Mozambique is one of the largest freshwater lake systems in all of Africa.

Namibia

Windhoek

The imposing statue is a representative of all Namibians who died in the struggle for independence from colonial rule.

Namibia, is set along the southwest coast of Africa and shares borders with Angola, Botswana and South Africa. Namibia was initially colonized by Germany; after WWI the nation was under the administration of the South African apartheid regime. A settler colony, Namibia fought a 24-year long struggle for liberation lead by the South West Africa People's Organization (SWAPO) which would end South African Apartheid rule in 1990. Namibians are of diverse ethnic origins. The principal groups are the Ovambo, Kavango, Herero, Himba, Damara. The majority of the population speak Oshiwambo languages specifically Nama and Damara. Khoisan groups are also represented in the region. The national language is English used by media outlets and the government.

Namibia is a developed nation, but you can still see the monuments that commemorate their liberation struggle and engage traditional culture as well. For starters, there is the Independence Memorial Museum, ahistorical museum in Windhoek, the capital. The museum commemorates Namibia's anti-colonial history and its liberation struggle.

Twyfelfontein is the site of the famous rock art concentrations in Africa with more than 5,000 petroglyphs and 200 rock paintings. And a trip to Katutura is where you can familiarize yourself with the local people and visit street markets.

Windhoek Hosea Kutako International Airport - Namibia

Hosea Kutako International Airport Chief Hosea Kutako

Hosea Kutako International Airport is the main international airport of Namibia, serving the capital city Windhoek.

Located well east of the city, 45 km, it is Namibia's largest airport with international connections. The airport was renamed 1990 is to honor Namibian national hero Hosea Kutako. Chief Hosea Komombumbi Kutako (1870 – 1970), was an early Namibian nationalist leader and a founder member of Namibia's first nationalist party, the South West African National Union (SWANU). Hosea Komombumbi Kutako was born in 1870 at Okahurimehi, in the Aminuis Reserve in Namibia. In

1920, Hosea Kutako was officially appointed as leader of the Herero people by Frederik Maharero. Hosea Kutako took over his role with a commitment to preserve the glory of the Herero before and during the German colonization, as well as of the atrocities in the Battle of Waterberg. The seat of his chieftaincy was situated at the settlement of Toasis in the Aminuis area.

In 1920, he founded the Green Flags, an association to preserve traditions,

Kutako became deputy chief of Namibia's Traditional Leaders Council, and also became Chief of the Botswana Mbanderu people in 1951. Along with the British Anglican priest Rev. Michael Scott, he submitted numerous petitions to the United Nations during the 1950s and 1960s calling on the world body to end South African rule and grant Namibia independence. This eventually led to the UN's recognition of Namibia as a sovereign country under colonial administration by South Africa and the historic 1971 advisory opinion of the International Court of Justice that South Africa's continued administration of Namibia was illegal in terms of international law. Hosea Kutako is considered a national hero inNamibia.

Hosea Kutako is one of nine national heroes of Namibia that wereidentified at the inauguration of the country's Heroes' Acre near Windhoek. 101

Niger

Niamey

The country of Niger is located in Western Africa. Niger is insulated by its regional neighbors Nigeria, Libya, Chad, Burkina Faso, Mali and Algeria. The nation is named after the Niger River. The country is also multiethnic comprised of the Hausa, Zarma, Songhai, Kanouri, Taureg, Fulani, Toubou and Arab groups. Most groups speak their indigenous languages; the national language is French. Colonized by the French, Niger declared its independence in 1960.

Niger is a large country, so there's a great deal to see starting with the capital, Niamey, the heart of the nation. As well as Agadez, with its 1,000 years of Sahelian camel caravans, previously a part of the Songhai Empire. Ayorou, has numerous mosques and marketplaces to visit. Nguigmi, Tahoua are cities where you can see various groups trading goods. However, one of the most magical places in the county is Timia a real-life oasis town in the middle of the desert, here you can engage the traditional villagers of the region.

Nigeria

Lagos Abuja

Niger is on the Gulf of Guinea, and shares borders with Cameroon, Chad, Niger and Benin. One of the most populous nations on the African continent it has over 200 ethnic groups. Hausa, Fulani, Yoruba, Igbo (Ibo), Ijaw, Kanuri, Ibibio, and Tiv just to name a few. Most of the population speaks their indigenous languages like Hausa, Yoruba, Igbo (Ibo), Fulani, and over 500 additional other languages. The national language is English typically expressed as Pidgin English. Colonized by the British the nation declared its independence through a peaceful transfer of power in 1960.

Worth seeing while in Nigeria is the Zuma Rock, outside the capital of Abuja. Traditional culture and historical sites are Calabar Museum. Calabar was once a primary slave trading port in West Africa. Lagos, the largest city in Nigeria, showcases Olumo Rock. This location has a great cultural museum, a craft shop for local artworks, and caves that revisit the history of the Ogun region as a whole. Ibadan, the capital of the Oyo Empire, is an attraction for practitioners of the Ifa tradition.

Murtala Muhammed International Airport - Nigeria

Murtala Muhammed International Airport

General Murtala Ramat Muhammed

Murtala Muhammed International Airport is an international airport located in Ikeja, Lagos State, Nigeria. The airport was initially built during World War II and is named after Murtala Mu-hammed, the fourth military ruler of Nigeria. General

Murtala Ramat Muhammed, referred to as Nigeria's unforgettable leader was a Nigerian Army general who was 4th Head of State of Nigeria from 1975 until his assassination in 1976. Here are the major achievements that he gained as president, in just a matter of a year before he was assassinated:

- He initiated a comprehensive review of the Third National Development Plan. Singling out inflation as the greatest danger to theeconomy.103
- He started the reorganization and demobilization of 100,000 troops from the armed forces. The number of troops in the armed forces decreased from 250,000 to 150,000.
- He implemented a mass purge in the Nigerian civil service. A retrenchment exercise was implemented as part of a strategy to refocus theservice.
- Mohammed created new states and renamed others, he also put in place plans to build a new Federal Capital Territory due to Lagos being overcrowded. The states he created include Bauchi, Benue, Borno, Imo, Niger, Ogun, and Ondo. This brought the total number of states in Nigeria to 19 in 1976.
- He introduced plans to build a new Federal Capital Territory due to Lagos being overcrowded. He set up a panel headed by Justice Akinola Aguda, which chose the Abuja area as the new capital ahead of other proposed locations.

Nigeria's former High Commissioner in Namibia Ambassador Adegboyega Christopher Ariyo described him as down-to-earth and a well-disciplined soldier. "He jolted a sleeping nation into life. The vibrancy in his voice was arresting. The fire in his eyes charmed and awed the nation. He adopted a low-profile policy," he said. Unfortunately, his time in the office was short, but his memories remain so vivid in the hearts and minds of Nigerians.

Rwanda

Liberation Day Monument

Kigali

The small East African country shares the region with the Democratic Republic of the Congo, Uganda and Tanzania. The nation was colonized by both Germany and Belgium, establishing its independence in 1962. The largest ethnic groups in Rwanda are the Hutus, which are a majority, the Tutsis and Twa.

In Nyanza experience the period of Rwandan royalty at the ancient King'sPalace, it was the capital of the nation's pre-colonial past. Lake Kivu this site has several attractions it ranges from Gisenyi in the north to the multicultural island of Ishwa in the south. Elevated fishing villages, clusters of trademark catamaran skiffs on the water. Nyanza is also the home of the Rwesero Art Museum on of the most prominent in the country. Finally, there are number of genocide memorial sites, such as Murambi, Gisozi, Gisenyi, Nyamata, Bisesero, Nyarubuye, Ntarama and Nyanza Memorials

Senegal

African Renaissance Monument Dakar

The African Renaissance Monument was erected by Senegal's President Abdoulaye Wade as a symbol of Senegal's independence from France.

The Monument is a tall copper statue located on top of one of the twinhills known as Collines des Mamelles, outside Dakarin Senegal. The monument is built overlooking the Atlantic Ocean and was designed by the Senegalese architect Pierre Goudiaby. It symbolizes the triumph of African liberation and rivals the Statue of Liberty and the Eiffel Tower as a tour-ist destination.

Senegal is the western tip of the African continent. Its regional neighbors are Gambia, Guinea,

ethnic group is the Wolof, followed by Fula andinka and Soninke. Wolof, an indigenous cial sectors, however the national language France in 1960.

useum of African Arts, and the famous Dutch fort on Goree Island, accessed by ferry boats. Just north of Dakar, the city of Saint-Lou-is hosts a famous jazz festival every May. The Great Mosque is in Touba, the spiritual center of the Mouride order of Sufis, Also, home of the tomb of Mouride founder, Sufi scholar, and teacher. 106

Seychelles

Victoria

The Zonm Lib: The statue of a man breaking free of chains, installed in 1978, marks the country's struggle for independence on 'Liberation Day' of June 5, 1977.

The island nation sits in the Indian Ocean off the coast of East Africa. It was colonized by both the British and French declaring its independence in 1976. The major ethnic groups in Seychelles are the Seychellois, which is Creole. The national language is French. One of the world's most beautiful tropical destinations with the best beaches to match, this archipelago nation has 115 islets scattered in the Indian Ocean.

Some of the major islands to visit, are Praslin and Mahe which are the most frequented, then Silhouette Island, Beau Vallon, Cap Ternay and La Digue. If you're there for the beaches and want to see something rare, visit Grand Anse Island which has yellow-white sand and is the longest beach in the Seychelles. To get a little history in while there visit the capital city of Victoria which houses the Island nations' National Museum. 107

Sierra Leone

Liberation Monument

Freetown

Sierra Leone officially the Republic of Sierra Leone, informally Salone, is a country on the southwest coast of West Africa. It is bordered by Liberia to the southeast and Guinea to the north-east. The capital and largest city is Freetown. The country is divided into five administrative regions which are subdivided into sixteen districts. Sierra Leone is a constitutional Republic with a unicameral parliament, and a directly elected president. Sierra Leone achieved independence from Britain on 27 April 1961, led by Milton Margai who became the country's first Prime Minister Sierra Leone held its first general election as an independent nation on May 27, 1962. On 19 April 1971, Stevens' government abolished Sierra Leone's parliamentary system and declared Sierra Leone a presidential republic. Sixteen ethnic groups inhabit Sierra Leone, with the two largest and most influential being the Temne and Mende people. About 2% the country's population are the Krio people, who are descendants of freed African American and West Indian slaves. The Krio is the most widely spoken language across Sierra Leone. Sierra Leone is a major producer of diamond, titanium, bauxite, and gold, and it has one of the world's largest deposits of rutile.

Somalia

Mogadishu

The Independence Monument is actually just a little bit out of Hargeisa. It is a hand holding a detailed map of Somaliland.

This East African country sits on the Indian Ocean coast, and shares borders with Kenya and Ethiopia. The country was colonized by both France and Italy gaining its independence in 1960. Somalians typically identify themselves by clan, of which there are several, the Isaaq, Hawiya, Dir, Darod, Digil Rahanweyn, and the Mirifle Rahanweyn. Somali is the official language of Somalia. In terms of origin, the Somali language is African-Asiatic belonging to the Cushitic branch of languages. Arabic is also considered a national language.

Places to go, Sa'ad ad-Din Island has become one of the country's rare national parks, the Island is another part of the beautiful Zeila Archipelago. The ancient city of Iskushuban has beautiful arabesque fortifications from centuries ago. The main attraction is the waterfalls, which is the second largest in the country. Lamadaya, is also known for its waterfalls. 109

South Africa

Johannesburg -Cape Town- Durban -Pretoria

At the tip of southern Africa, the nation of South Africa shares the region with Namibia, Botswana, Swaziland and Lesotho. Home the world's most famous political prisoner turned president, Nelson Mandela, and legendary military strategist and general Shaka Zulu. South Africa liberated itself from the Apartheid regime of white minority rule in 1994.

It will take several trips to experience everything South Africa has to offer, but for starters there's Cape Town for the view of Table Mountain the famous flat, plateau- like topped mountain. The town has water trails, sports, and beaches as well as all of the modern trappings. Durban, which is climatically pleasant year around is an internationally popular holiday destination. Johannesburg or Jo'burg houses the Apartheid Museum a memorial that details the nations' struggle against the apartheid regime, the city also offers all trappings of any metropolis, like dining, night- life, entertainment, arts and shopping.

To experience the "real" South Africa, take a trip to Soweto and a host of traditional villages. Soweto is the center of the anti- apartheid struggle. Standard township tours should include Vilakazi Street, the early home of Nelson Mandela, Walter Sisulu Square where South Africa's Freedom Charter was signed in 1955, the Hector Pieterson Memorial, where the 1976 uprising began.

Traditional Villages you don't want to miss are Shakaland, an intro- duction to Zulu culture and traditions, where you can see the bee- hive homesteads and building methods and engage traditional beadwork and pottery making. Shakaland is one of the best-known cultural villages in the country. You can also get some traditional Zulu beer and stay the night in the beehive trans- formed into modernized hotels. Other traditional villages to visit are Simunye which is like, but smaller than DumaZulu. To experience a variety of southern African cultures in one place, visit Lesedi Village which will introduce you to the traditional practices of the Xhosa, Sotho, Venda, Ndebele and others. Last, but not least, is the Basotho cultural village near Golden Gate Highland National Park in Free State province.110

This village allows one to understand the historical timeline of the Sotho culture, with buildings of different eras staged in chronological order.

O. R. Tambo International Airport - South Africa

O.R. Tambo International Airport

Cde Oliver Reginald Kaizana Tambo

O.R. Tambo International Airport is South Africa's biggest airport located in Johannesburg, receiving an average of over 21 million passengers per annum. The airport was named after one of South Africa's most celebrated apartheid heroes, Cde Oliver Reginald Kaizana Tambo. He was a South African anti- apartheid politician and revolutionary who served as President of the African National Congress (ANC) from 1967 to 1991.

In 1943, Cde Tambo, Mandela, and Walter Sisulu founded the ANC Youth League, with Cde Tambo becoming its first National Secretary and a member of the National Executive in 1948. The Youth League proposed a change in the tactics of the anti-apartheid movement where they introduced their own "Programme of Action." This program advocated tactics such as boycotts, civil disobedience, strikes, and non-collaboration.

In 1958, he became Deputy President of the ANC and in 1959 was served with a five-year banning order by the government. He was exiled to London where he stayed, in the ANC, until he returned in 1990 as National Chairperson of theANC, after 30 years of exile. However, he could not be fit enough to be president after he had had a stroke in 1989. So, Nelson Mandela became president instead.

Cde Tambo was directly responsible for organizing active guerilla units. Along with his comrades Nelson Mandela, Joe Slovo, and Walter Sisulu, he directed and facilitated several attacks against the apartheid state.

Tambo established residences in Zambia and London, England, among other locales, and received party aid from some European countries, including Holland, East Germany, and the Soviet Union to provide shelter for resistance.

From abroad Tambo coordinated resistance and guerrilla movements, and, despite internal organizational struggles, was able to keep the multiracial ANC intact.

Cde Oliver Reginald Kaizana Tambo remains an iconic figure in South Africa and to all Black descendants for the significant role that he played during apartheid in fighting the oppressor and liberating South Africa's president instead.

Republic of South Sudan

Juba

The Republic of South Sudan is a landlocked country in East Central Africa. It is bordered to the east by Ethiopia, to the north by Sudan, to the west by theCentral African Republic, to the south-west by Democratic Republic of the Congo, to the south by Uganda and to the southeast by Kenya. Its capital and largest city is Juba. It includes the vast swamp region of the Sudd, formed by the White Nile and known locally as the Bahr al Jabal meaning "Mountain Sea". Sudan was occupied by Egypt under the Muhammad Ali dynasty and was governed asanAnglo-Egyptian condominium until Sudanese independence in 1956. South Sudan became an independent state from the Republic of the Sudan on9 July 2011, following the January 2011 referendum. South Sudan is a multilingual country, with 60 indigenous languages spoken in the country. South Sudan has a population of 12 million, mostly of the Nilotic peoples, and it is demographically among the youngest nations in the world, with roughly half under 18 years old. The country is a member of the United Nations, the African Union, the East African Community, the Intergovernmental Authority on Development and is a party to the Geneva Conventions

Sudan

Khartoum-Omdurman

Part of East Africa, Sudan shares borders with South Sudan, Cen-tral African Republic, Chad, Libya and Egypt. Formerly a British colony the nation gained independence from the British in 1956. Sudan is both multi-ethnic and multi-lingual with approximately

20 major ethnic groups; The largest ones being Sudanese-Arab, Nubian, Copts, Zahawa or Beri, Masaut, Fulani and Beja. Indigenous languages are primary for most; however, English is the nations' official language, Arabic is a working language.

Sudan holds numerous monuments of the ancient world. Just to name a few; The center of the ancient Napata Kingdom, Meroe. Next, Khartoum, where the two strands of the River Nile meet before heading north to Nubia and Egypt. Kerma, is also an important ancient site along the Nile. The Western Deffufa, one of the largest and oldest worshipping houses in the world. The Deffufa is surrounded by burial complexes and unearthed monuments of Nubian deities believed to be at least 5,000 years old. And finally, Jabal Naqa, just outside of the capital at Khartoum, are numerous temples most notably the Temple of Amun, dedicatedto the Egyptian deity Amun Ra.

Tanzania

Dar Es Salaam

The East African country sits on the coast of the Indian Ocean and shares borders with Somalia, Mozambique, Democratic Republic of Congo, Uganda and Kenya. Colonized by the British, the nation declared its independence in 1964. Like many African nations, Tanzania is multiethnic with over a hundred different groups, some of the dominant groups are the Sukuma a Bantu-ethnic group the Nyamwezi, Chagga, Haya, Hadza and the Maasai who also reside in

nearby Kenya. Each ethnic group has its own unique language.The nation was colonized by the British and declared its independence in 1964.

Sudan

Khartoum-Omdurman

Part of East Africa, Sudan shares borders with South Sudan, Cen-tral African Republic, Chad, Libya and Egypt. Formerly a British colony the nation gained independence from the British in 1956. Sudan is both multi-ethnic and multi-lingual with approximately

21 major ethnic groups; The largest ones being Sudanese-Arab, Nubian, Copts, Zahawa or Beri, Masaut, Fulani and Beja. Indigenous languages are primary for most; however, English is the nations' official language, Arabic is a working language.

Sudan holds numerous monuments of the ancient world. Just to name a few; The center of the ancient Napata Kingdom, Meroe. Next, Khartoum, where the two strands of the River Nile meet before heading north to Nubia and Egypt. Kerma, is also an important ancient site along the Nile. The Western Deffufa, one of the largest and oldest worshipping houses in the world. The Deffufa is surrounded by burial complexes and unearthed monuments of Nubian deities believed to be at least 5,000 years old. And finally, Jabal Naqa, just outside of the capital at Khartoum, are numerous temples most notably the Temple of Amun, dedicated to the Egyptian deity Amun Ra.

Tanzania

Dar Es Salaam

The East African country sits on the coast of the Indian Ocean and shares borders with Somalia, Mozambique, Democratic Republic of Congo, Uganda and Kenya. Colonized by the British, the nation declared its independence in 1964.
Like many African nations, Tanzania is multiethnic with over a hundred different groups, some of the dominant groups are the Sukuma a Bantu-ethnic group the Nyamwezi, Chagga, Haya, Hadza and the Maasai who also reside in nearby Kenya. Each ethnic group has its own unique language.

The nation was colonized by the British and declared its independence in 1964.

Tanzania is full of natural sites, just to name a few, Mount Kiliman- jaro in Mount Kilimanjaro National Park, Mount Meru, the fifth highest in all of Africa and Arusha, originally founded by the Maasai, is the definition of natural abundance. On Zanzibar Island (aka Ungoga), which is actually a string of islands, there's Stone Town, Nungwi, Matemwe, Jambiani and Bwejuu where the natural beauty lies in the numerous beaches.

Julius Nyerere International Airport - Tanzania

Julius Nyerere International Airport

President Julius Kambarage Nyerere

The Julius Nyerere International Airport is Tanzania's biggest airport, located in the country's capital, Nairobi. It was named after its former president, the late Julius Kambarage Nyerere. He was a Tanzanian anti-colonial activist, politician, and political theorist. He governed Tanganyika as Prime Minister from 1961 to 1962 and then as President from 1963 to 1964, after which he led its successor state, Tanzania, as President from 1964 to 1985. A founding member of the Tanganyika African National Union (TANU) party—which in 1977 became the Chama Cha Mapinduzi party—he chaired it until 1990. 121

Ideologically an African nationalist and African socialist, he pro- moted a political philosophy known as Ujamaa. In 1954, he helped form TANU, through which he campaigned for Tanganyikan independence from the British Empire. Cde Nyerere preached a non- violent protest to achieve this aim. Elected to the Legislative Council in the 1958–1959 elections, Nyerere then led TANU to victory at the 1960 general election, becoming Prime Minister. Negotiations with the British authorities resulted in Tan-ganyikan independence in 1961.Here are some of his major accomplishments:

- One of the achievements of Cde Nyerere was toning down eth- nicity in Tanzania. Tanzania has KiSwahili as a national language. He used this to unify the people of Tanzania, being a nation with 120 tribes, not to mention subtribes.
- He led TANU to victory at the 1960 general election, becoming Prime Minister where he negotiated with the British authorities resulting in Tanganyikan independence in 1961.

"Simplicity - is the only word I can find to describe him with. Julius Nyerere was the first President of Tanzania who insisted on being called a Mwalimu –teacher. He declined titles, privileges and enjoyed the simple life even as President of Tanzania. When he retired, he went back to his small village to live a simplelife

–attending Holy Mass every day," said Professor Father Juvenalis Baitu, former Deputy Vice-Chancellor of the Catholic University of Eastern Africa (CUEA). He knew Cde Nyerere on a personal level. 122

Togo

Lome

The beautiful Independence Monument was built as a tribute to Togo's independence from France on April 27, 1960. The structure is composed of a human silhouette carved within it and surrounded by promenades, palm trees, manicured lawns, fountains, and a black gold iron fence.

This West African nation sits on the Atlantic Ocean coast, it shares borders with Ghana, Benin, and Niger. The country was colonized by both Germany and France gaining its independence in 1960. There are around 40 ethnic groups in Togo. The largest groups are the Ewe, then Kotokoli, Tchamba, Kabye and a host of smaller groups, most of which speak their indigenous languages. The national language is French.

Although one of the smaller countries on the African continent, Togo has its share of sites to see. Lome, the capital, is busy and has countless markets. For a taste of the culture, the traditional villages of Koutammakou also called the 'Land of the Batammariba' has rustic villages built from adobe walls and thatched roofs. The village offers a glimpse into traditional life along with the natural aesthetic of mountain-topped horizons and fertile bush lands.

Togoville, the small city is named after the nation, is known for its traditional Voodoo shrines and mud brick structures. And the small town of Atakpame and its little basin in the midst of the impossibly green Atakora Mountain is the site of a historic battle. During the precolonial period two of West Africa's greatest empires, Oyo and the Ashanti engaged in an epic clash here. Today, this location is still a center, but for traditional markets and trading.

Tunisia

Tunis

Tunisia is located in North Africa; its regional neighbors are Alge-ria and Libya. Colonized by the French, Tunisia declared its independence in 1956. Although, by many accounts Tunisia is said to be largely homogenous being Arab-Berber, there is also a minority population called the Amazigh Tunisia's original indigenous population who have suffered from near erasure by Arabisation of the country, therefore, the national is Arabic.

The capital city of Tunis, that has a French side and the Maghreb side. Another major attraction in Tunisia is the El Djem, an amphitheater with large elliptical arches, a relic of the ancient world. Also, Tozeur, an oasis settlement in the desert, dominated by the Berber tradition.

Uganda

Kampala

The Uganda Independence Monument is a towering concrete sculpture located in downtown Kampala.

Located in southern Africa, the nation shares borders with Kenya, Tanzania, the Democratic Republic of the Congo and South Sudan. Colonized by the British the nation declared its independence in 1962. The largest ethnic group in Uganda is the Baganda, followed by the Banyankole, Basoga, Bakiga, Iteso, Langi Acholi, Bagisua and Lugbara, just to name a few. Most groups speak their indigenous language although English is used nationally.

A host of places to visit, first the capital city Kampala, which is the ancestralhome of the Buganda kingdom. Everything from ancient relics of the Kasubi Tombs to busy city life can be found in Kampala. Looking for relaxing beaches? There's Uganda's archipelago, the Ssese Islands, the most popular ones being Bug-gala and Bulago. One natural site worth seeing before you leave Uganda is Mount Elgon and the famous summit of Wagagai, a volcano that is among the highest in Africa and believed to be.

Zambia

Lusaka

In front of the government offices in downtown Lusaka stands the Zambian Freedom Statue. The artwork depicts a man break-ing free from chains, representing the struggles Zambians faced while overthrowing the chains of colonialism.

Located in southern Africa, Zambia shares borders with the Democratic Republic of the Congo, Tanzania, Mozambique, Botswana, Namibia and Angola. Colonized by the British the nation declared its independence in 1964.

Zambia has a host of natural sites that are worth seeing, first Mosioa- Tunya the second-largest cataract and the most striking point of Victoria Falls. Blue Lagoon National Park, just outside of Lusaka and Kafue Flats, this vast floodplain of a reserve swings between desert in the dry season and fertile watering hole once the rainy season returns. Solwezi is home of the country's oldest Stone Age engravings, are hidden in the caves and canyons along the Kifubwa River. To get the taste of Zambian traditional culture visit Musokotwane, home of the Tokaleya people.

Zimbabwe

Nehanda Charwe Nyakasikana, more widely known as Mbuya (grandmother in Shona) Nehanda, was hanged in 1898 for leading an anti-colonial rebellion. She was an influential spirit medium who rallied people to fight against the seizure of their land by colonialists.

Harare Bulawayo

National Heroes Acre or simply Heroes Acre is a burial ground and national monument in Harare, Zimbabwe.

Zimbabwe is located in the southeast corner of the African continent. The country's regional neighbors are Mozambique, South Africa, Botswana, Zambia and the Democratic Republic of Congo. Home of the last Pan Africanist from the era of independence, former president Robert Mugabe. The nation was colonized bythe British and formerly known as Rhodesia. Zimbabweans fought a long-armed struggle, which lead to a victory and a declaration of independence in 1980. The population is divided among two groups, the Shona, who are a majority and the Ndebele, a minority. Although most Zimbabweans are Bantu-speaking, though English is the common language, a linguistic relic of its colonialpast.

Harare, with nearly three million people is not only the capital but also the largest city in the nation. The city sits on a plateau in Zimbabwe's central highlands. Aside from the aesthetic,Harare holds a great deal of history, the city is also the host of the National Gallery, and the NationalArchives. Zimbabwe has a wealth of cultural, natural and historical sites; Most important, Great Zimbabwe, located within Masvingo.

Great Zimbabwe is a great complex that is believed to be at least 700 years old and denotes the dry architectural capabilities of ancient African civilizations in this region. Another natural site, Highveld is comprised of hills of dolomite rock and suspended boulders, that is believed to be at least 1800 meters above sea level. Chinhoyi another natural site, is famed mainly for its caves that are carved into the cliffs in the backdrop of the city. And finally, to engage traditional cultures and people, visit Monde Village, where you will meet the local people, and engage the culture, customs and the history of Zimbabwe.

Robert Mugabe International Airport - Zimbabwe

Robert Mugabe International Airport Mr President Robert Gabriel Mugabe

The Robert Mugabe International Airport is located in Harare, the Capital of Zimbabwe. The airport was named after the country's former president who governed for nearly four decades. The late Cde Robert Mugabe was a Zimbabwean revolutionary who served as First Secretary of the Zimbabwe African National Union (ZANU) from 1975 to 1980; and then as the country's Prime Minister from 1980 to 1987. He then led ZANU's successor party ZANU - Patriotic Front from the year 1987 to 2017. Angered by the white minority rule of his homeland within the British Empire, Cde Mugabe embraced Marxism and joined African nationalists calling for an independent state controlled by the Black majority. After making anti-government comments, he was convicted of sedition and imprisoned between 1964 and 1974. After he was released, Cde Mugabe went to Mozambique, led ZANU, and over-saw its role in the Rhodesian Bush War, fighting Ian Smith's pre-dominantly white government. He is a well-decorated liberator who led his party against Ian Smith, leading to the freedom of Zimbabwe.

- He was the first secretary of the ZANU party which fought and won the war against Ian Smith, leading to the liberation ofZimbabwe.
- He introduced Free Education for All, Health for All in 1980 which allowed all Zimbabweans to have free access to medical treatment andeducation.
- Cde Robert Mugabe initiated the Land Reform program in 2000 that resulted in most Zimbabwean families who had lost their lands to colonialists restore them.

- Cde Mugabe belonged to a group of nationalists such as the late Vice- President Joshua Mqabuko Nkomo, Cdes Jason Ziyaphapha Moyo, George Silundika, and Herbert Chitepo among others, who sacrificed their lives to liberate the country.
- He devoted his entire life to fighting against white imperialism. Up to this day, the country is free of racism and racial inequalities thanks to his boldness and diligence in fighting against white supremistideology.

He was a distinguished revolutionary who will always remain the country's icon despite circumstances surrounding his retirement. Cde Mugabe's illustrious record could not be expunged from the history of Zimbabwe.

Thank you for reading and for your interest.

What Mr. Victor Green thoughtfully started decades ago, we have expanded and grown. The global green book exists so that we can live fearlessly with a peace of mind, knowing precisely where safe spaces are no matter where we are inthe world. Our future depends on it. Please add to our list andstay tuned. Your future depends on it.

Global Green Book | Healthcare Edition-2021

info@iloveblackpeople.com | +1 202-558-5143

Made in the USA
Middletown, DE
11 February 2022